HOW TO **LOVE** OTHERS WITHOUT LOSING **YOURSELF**

Five Powerful Steps to Snap out of Your Pain, Find Your True Self and Make Your Relationships Awesome

Analay Souza Campos

To my mother,

Mom, there is an *end* to suffering and pain.

And I found it.

I love you *forever*.

MY GIFT TO YOU

Download a FREE printable version
of the Five Steps Daily Reminder

www.analaysouzacampos.com/gift

Contents

Preface

This book is the first thing in my life I can call a contribution. One of my first actions that is not an attempt to receive or to elicit love and acceptance from others. Instead, this book is about sharing my perfectly imperfect nature and hoping it can inspire you to do the same.

I'm a recovering codependent.

Codependency is an excessive emotional or psychological reliance on a partner, typically one who requires support on account of an illness or addiction.

I'm going through divorce after being married for seven years. The most difficult and eye-opening seven years of my life. A full soul-cycle dedicated to learning about myself, and the deepest pathways of my heart.

I hope you can apply some of what I have learned through the most impactful journey of my life. I attended **Date with Destiny** with **Tony Robbins** about a month ago, and I have rewritten my destiny, my blueprint, and regained the power of my soul. I pray that my experience and breakthroughs help you reach your next level, whatever that is for you. I pray it helps you break free from your past and unleash your future.

Many men and women out there already have a loving and caring partner. I had the perfect partner for evolution purposes, let's put it that way. Since then, and with a lot of work and effort, I've come to a realization, and I've learned some lessons. I share these lessons here with the hope that they can put a spark in your heart. To get you searching for your ultimate fulfillment and true giving love. I believe there is a higher purpose for the light I have received, and that is to share it with you.

That is why I have written this book in 27 days. I've channeled real love for everyone that desires to wake up in their relationships by truly finding themselves.

If you want to take a stab at massive self-transformation, pretend you don't know yourself fully when you read this book.

Free yourself from having to ask every second if it applies or not to you. It's your mind stepping in. Give in. Let it grow deeper. Like no one is looking.

Like not even yourself is looking.

I have become this book. I have evolved into a woman who loves and accepts herself. I can now contribute from a place of abundance and eternal love.

At the end of yourself, is others.

I have unleashed my human and my divine nature writing these thoughts. I have channeled some of this content in a state of self-hypnosis. Some parts were written in deep emotional states of understanding and realization. I have come out as pure and authentic as I could be with myself.

Duality expresses itself throughout the book. Each chapter has a bit about my personal experience, thoughts, feelings, and struggles. I will open up about the journey back to my heart, and all that it took from myself and others to finally succeed in this quest. I will dive into the relevant painful experiences that propelled me to self-discovery.

In the same way, chapters also hold higher content and principles. These principles will free you from who you were and who you have been in your life up to now. These are the *Words of Wisdom* sections you will find throughout the book. Each chapter is like two of me talking. The human and the divine together on a journey to reintegration.

Besides the personal experience and the *Words of Wisdom* sections, you will find a third section called *Affirmations of Power*. These affirmations kept me going on the days of disbelief. They are the words I trust and tell myself on a daily basis to keep my duality integrated and renovated.

This book is not about me, but about what you can achieve for yourself. I pray that you find the ideas I have channeled here useful. And I hope the content invites you to revisit it from time to time.

Thank you for trusting me with your attention and the most delicate and vulnerable part of yourself.

Start with me on this path toward self-love and healing. It's been a dark, long road to myself, but, oh, so worth it.

What You Will Learn

These are the Five Steps I have identified so we can learn to love from freedom. Help me explore and dive into each step, discovering the secrets to mastering them and applying them as we walk through this journey together.

The Five Powerful Steps to Recover Your *True Identity* and Learn to Love *from Freedom*

STEP 1: **Break *free* from your *pain.*** Liberate yourself from the internal discomfort that has you coming back to a place of lack and misery. A feeling that you hurt because of external people or circumstances.

STEP 2: **Forgive yourself for what you did, not *who you are.*** Whether you regret events and decisions that have come to pass, learn to recognize that the real you is not attached to your history. Therefore, changing is not really changing yourself, but adjusting your focus to a clearer vision of who you really are.

STEP 3: **See others for *who they are*, not what they have done.** In past, current, or future relationships, you see others as you see yourself. Learn to see others through the filter of understanding and forgiveness and what that really entails.

STEP 4: **Learn to love yourself *completely*.** Develop the realization that cherry-picking the pieces of yourself you truly admire will never erase the totality of your human side. Integration and realization can only come from a place of self-love and self-acceptance. Learn to finally materialize a self-love feeling that lasts.

STEP 5: **Discover *abundance* within**. Embrace the notion that abundance is a place within yourself that cannot be created, only re-discovered. Learn to tap into the source of all love and fulfillment, so you can finally love yourself and others fully.

After diving into these steps and concepts, you will come out on the other side with a deeper understanding of what it takes to change your life and the love you give and receive for a much higher and fulfilling version of them all. You will master the art of truly loving others without getting lost in them. You will be free to love, and will not feel imprisoned by the love of others.

Let Go

~ Breathe in the emotion you want to create. ~

It is hard to give up control.

It is hard to say, "That's it, I'm done." When we struggle, it's particularly difficult. Leaving the fight, not answering back, not having the last word. It is hard to give up and desist on the life-long quest for love.

And maybe the reason why it is hard is because after it all, we had good intentions. We wanted the love, we wanted the happiness, we wanted to make someone else happy, give them a life. What could have been better than that?

Giving up control of the situation could take years. Yet, there comes a moment when the pain builds up at such a level that life forces us to retire from the race. These reasons that life gives us are often more painful than the situation we were experiencing in the first place.

An accident, the death of a child or family member, an act of violence, and so many more difficult trials. All indications that we should step back and reconsider what is it we are doing with our lives by continuing along in this quest of ours.

Even if your life is not like this in all areas, it is likely it follows a similar pattern in the areas you struggle with the most. Maybe it is time to step aside for just a bit and consider there might be a way we can avoid the ultimate pain that comes from being pushed to learn the lesson at the end of the trial. Maybe there is a way to successfully let go and find yourself before life forces you to.

I believe we can. I do not want you to learn from my lessons, because that would be impossible. But I hope to share some thoughts that can be useful in your life and your journey.

Let the guard down for a minute, and consider this: Maybe there is a way to let go that can still help you achieve the same results you have been incessantly *fighting* for.

Facing Ourselves

You wanted to be happy, right? Love, be loved and be happy as a result. Had you asked me when I was five years old what happiness was, that would have been my answer. What is it with us adult humans, that we enjoy complicating things? We often add so much *humanness* that we end up devaluing our experiences. Why do we contaminate our interactions with so many big words with empty meanings?

Words have a serious impact on our own internal experience of the world. What we say to ourselves about a certain experience is what determines how we will relive that experience in the future. Think about it. Can you remember an experience in your life that felt pretty damn good, yet you had a thought to yourself that now, when you retrieve it, you have to deal with over and over?

Yes. And that is how we live. We live with a vision of the world we have not experienced but have told ourselves that's how we should interpret it. This interpretation is done, every second, by contrasting our real-life experiences with our beliefs and values, and the meaning and rules we have for each of them.

Match them, and we have real happiness. Find a mismatch and "Umm, that wasn't at all what I expected." Have a total mismatch, and you call that hell.

There is nothing wrong with me, or with you, or with him. Happy humans have taken the time to understand the duality within them. They have forgiven themselves and have started the journey back to their oneness, their reintegration. The integration of the human side with the divine side we all have in us.

Have you ever heard two voices talking to you within? I'm sure you have, as I have. How many times have we chosen one over the other consciously? How many times have we pretended the one we disagree with is not there? Have we ever really made an unconscious decision? Could it be that we fool ourselves into believing things just happened to us, and we didn't know better?

As horrible as our human lives can get, can we really claim we are victims of our own destinies?

What I have discovered is that we tend to listen to the selfish voice. Because we truly believe that acting according to its principles will meet a need we desperately need met. And we would sacrifice anything in that moment to feel whole, thinking that it would take us to a feeling of completeness and happiness.

Yet, most of the times we find that when we meet the need, it does not last long enough. It's like a taste of our destiny, but through the wrong means, so it dissipates—it fades.

So, what is a divine soul with good intentions, wanting to love and be loved, doing in this world? Feeling like a failure, and truly struggling to love and feel loved? Why do we struggle so much to create what we truly want?

I asked myself this for years.

I restarted my life many times with the conviction that each time was "it." That I knew what was missing. And that now that I had it, I would never let it go. My life would be different and now love would finally show up for me.

Do you know anyone like that? Have you felt like this before? If you have, you probably experienced the immense emptiness that comes when you realize that after moving heaven and earth, not only are you not fulfilled, but those around you aren't either.

By now you might have even formed a family. If you are lucky, a home. And detangling the circus that you have created in the name of fulfillment is not so easily dissolved. We often dwell in sadness and depression, telling ourselves we deserve it. And take our own punishment to the grave. Not knowing these unresolved issues will have a detrimental impact on our children, partners, and others around us.

The ball will keep rolling, and the pattern will outlive you. Your children will take some with them, and unless they go through what they call "a life-defining moment," they might not realize it and live life halfway.

Wow, that was overwhelming, wasn't it? But let's face it, overwhelming why? Because these are the written words you have thought about and told yourself so many times but never dare to write or act upon?

I get you, and not only do I get you, I love you and deeply understand you. But do you love yourself? No, I mean, do you *really* love yourself? Sounds selfish, right? Loving yourself above all things. Would you consider this thought? That loving yourself is the least selfish thing you will ever do?

This book is a journey to learn to love yourself. It sounds easy, but do you know what that truly means? I'm not talking about booking a spa day and putting that above spending the day with your partner. I'm talking about getting a real understanding of what an emotional healthy version of you would do for yourself and your relationships. A fulfilled you. I realized after many years that if you are getting into a relationship looking to fulfill you, you have, my friend, gotten into a pretty rotten deal. The most outstanding relationships are between two fulfilled humans who came to share and give to each other. Not lacking, desperate humans looking to find what they cannot recognize first in themselves.

But, why? Why would we look for what we can't find within ourselves in others? And why—even worse—why would others feel so attracted to a *lacking* person? These are heavy questions. Often in a relationship where there is emotional blame, shame and lack of accountability, we can pinpoint the above patterns in at least one of the partners. If you find a relationship like this, that has lasted over three years, then you will most likely find that both partners present the pattern, otherwise they wouldn't have stayed together for that long. This pattern was not useless. It was serving the part of themselves which was so lacking in the first place.

I'm not an expert in human psychology, or the mind, by any means. But I'm an expert, with absolute certainty, in the illusion of pain and disappointment an *unfulfilled human* can generate for himself and others. I have been in the darkest places of the heart, mind, and soul. I have seen the conflict arise between the three of them. And watched the saddest movie of all times—all three incapable of seeing each other and aligning with love and compassion.

This book, as you might have guessed by now, is not about your partner. Yes, I know, he hurt you. Yes, I know your story is painful. Mine was, too. But I stopped the pattern of those who came before me, those who also had a pretty rough life but could only manage to *talk* about how hard life was, and never acting to fix what was broken. They kept reliving the same experience that hurt them so much. Even after the separation, they can still feel the attacks. Do you see what I mean? How could you still be so miserable if the inflicting side is already out of the picture? Where are those attacks really coming from?

If you want to explore that thought, this book is for you. If you really see yourself as the creator of an incredible, fulfilling destiny, then you also must learn to recognize you were partially the creator of your life up to this point.

I love you. Do you?

STEP ONE

Breaking *Free* from Your *Pain*

~ I was a prisoner until I realized my chains were made of leaves. ~

What would it mean to break free from pain? Breaking free presupposes we are somehow hostage or slave to some kind of unpleasant feeling that makes us *hurt*.

Pain manifests in many ways. Pain is suffering, sadness, depression. Pain is also attacks, violence, and frustration. Pain can be disguised as several human emotions. We justify some, and judge others. But pain is *pain*. It is a very powerful state of misery. And it will lead to more pain until a breakthrough takes place.

The notion that we are slaves to this pain is a human notion. We dwell in that feeling, in a way, because it serves us. Think about it. Why would we stay there otherwise? I know, to a person who is hurting, this idea might be hard to accept. Maybe even seem offensive. But we humans would not perpetuate a state like this—as painful and horrible as it can be—if we weren't satisfying one of our non-negotiable human needs.

> The slavery lies on the very need that drives us to stay in a situation that is uncomfortable to us.

We have all been there at one time or another in our lives. Those situations you know you should not have allowed, yet you seem to slip back into over and over with a vague excuse that things or people, somehow, will change on their own.

We all have an *old story*. This is the story we tell ourselves over and over in our heads, when our conscious mind wants to do something our heart does not fully agree with.

This is also the story we tell others to derive sympathy, and to justify our outcomes. Ultimately, this is the story we hate the most about ourselves, a self-pity story that our divine self has trouble believing.

We will call it *old* because we will discover it doesn't serve us. We will call it *old* because if you are reading this book, you already can see a new story for yourself.

Let's dive into the old story and what happens to us when we stay attached to it. Let's see how it comes to catch us even when we think we have broken free.

The *Old* Story

My *old* story is not important, neither is yours. There is a part of me that is afraid everything is lost. There is a part of me that, as I write right now, is sabotaging the divine plan my soul was created for. That part of myself is resisting to manifest my purpose. This part of you exists, too, and you must own it. I call that side of us: the monster. The side of us we often cannot recognize. The part of us which behaves in a way dominated by primal instincts. That knows how to hurt and feel hurt. The more you try to extinguish this side of you, the bigger it will get.

We start now. No waiting for your *monster* to settle. It will always be there. It's not about extinguishing your monster but giving it the love it is craving. Fall in love with your monster. Fall in love with that part of you that is hurting. It is demanding to feel loved and accepted.

Please, don't kill it. Don't run away from yourself in the name of loving someone else. You are sabotaging yourself and not loving yourself fully. I know, the monster in you is probably putting on a pretty rough show right now.

Notice. Take a minute of silence, focus on your breathing. See it. Feel it. What does it say to you? What do you tell yourself when you feel sad and defeated? What are you doing to yourself, in subtle ways, or in some cases, big ways, that are currently harmful to you, and why? And what are you doing to change this self-destructive treatment?

The point is that if you look closer, you will find patterns that are extreme in their own action. And then another extreme pattern right away to attempt to correct it. You try to feed the little, poor, unloved monster at some point before the day is over. You do that because, after all, you have been fighting with yourself not to give in all day. You do it in a negative way and then step back to correct it with a pretty harsh measure. A costly one.

It has taken a long time for me to discover the importance of loving myself. Not so much what loving myself looks like, but how to do it, and how to do it in a way that aligns with my purpose.

Love *every* part of *yourself*

We have been conditioned to hate the part of us that is desperately searching for love and acceptance. We try to push it away, we try to ignore it. And the painful truth is that the human part of us will never stop looking for it. We are innately created to need it. We will elicit the love in whatever way we can. We will do what it takes to find it in positive ways with positive habits. But if we don't get it, we will adopt self-destructive patterns to get it.

Perhaps this applies to you specifically and you are aware of it. Perhaps you feel this doesn't apply to you at all, and you are somewhat bothered when you read this. I invite you to watch yourself closely and consider the idea that not all of you is loved by you. Or you wouldn't experience suffering. I can now see the part of me that is totally neglected and begging desperately for love. I can see how much harm I'm doing to myself on a daily basis when I let a part of me indulge in a self-pity pool of thoughts and feelings.

How do we get that part of ourselves to budge into our new life plan? How do we tell that part of us there is satisfaction, love, and acceptance down the line? It wants to feel the love now, it wants to feel accepted now. And by the way, know that when I write this, I'm exactly at this point in my own journey. I'm figuring this out as I go, from my heart, and this deep desire to find myself, as I was born to be.

My story is not *important*, because it hasn't taken me to where *I want to be*.

My story is not important because, even if a small part of me believes it, it will make me indulge in self-destructive behaviors which will stir me away from the path to my new story.

Your story is not important because it is not about *you*, it's rather about what has *happened* to you.

And while you keep revisiting those facts, it will only take you back to your past, feeding the fear in the little child that still dwells within you.

Taking responsibility for your past does not mean you must continue living it. Owning your decisions up until now does not mean you must conform to a life that does not match your new blueprint.

Stop for a moment, drink a glass of water even if you had some recently. Do it and trust how much I love the human you are today, right now. Trust me, because we are well on our way to fully allowing ourselves to receive the love we *deserve,* and not only the love we *crave.*

Accepting and Releasing

Oh, my! That old story was my biggest asset. I would construct it bigger and bigger, amplify it, so I could appear more lovable to others. So that I would love myself once and for all through the acceptance and validation of others. I was convinced that by being a super giving woman to someone who didn't really value me, my worth would somehow increase. These were the thoughts that controlled me and defined my life until now.

Wow. That was a lot right there. How crazy and messed up is that? Can you begin to grasp the level of sophistication we are dealing with here? This is not standard lack of self-love. This is lack of self-love combined with a desperate need to find real love. There was only one way to get there. Total honesty and authenticity with myself first.

Sticking to my old story made me miserably lovable at times. It gave me a few moments of compassion here and there, none of which I enjoyed. I wasn't happy with myself. Either I was *amplifying* a problem to get more love, or I was *minimizing* a problem to be the hero. But I would tell myself I was lucky to have the chance to be loved at least in this way. I believed sacrifice and self-inflicted emotional pain were the means to get there.

Such was the pain and anxiety I lived with most of my life until now. My old story was this: I'm so giving to others, but yet they don't value me. It was also an unconscious excuse not to do more for myself. I thought of myself as really generous and dedicated to others, those whom I wanted to receive love from, that is. And then, when I didn't get the love and response I wanted, I would pity myself and cry to them in desperation. A sacrificing mother, a sacrificing wife, a hard worker. The one who does not have time to even go get a pedicure. Sound familiar? You get the point.

A complete slave of my deep need for love with the ignorance of not knowing how to get it.

Words of Wisdom

When you want to get something done, do you focus on why you can't do it, or do you find a way to do it? When you want to unleash massive action, do you go back and dwell on how horrible your life has been to this point, and all the things that prevented you from achieving your dreams? Or do you wonder if this is your time, after all, and go get it?

Let me share a secret with you: Your time is *never,* and your time is *always*. It only takes a shift in your focus. I know it is easier said than done. I dwelled in self-pity for a long time. And you know what? It was such elegant, subtle self-pity it was very hard to recognize and snap out of. I would never have called myself one of those self-pitying women, yet there was little or no progress in my life. For years, I felt I was deviating more and more from my inner light in the name of loving others.

Trust me, self-pity takes you to a place of blame and regret, to a place of projection and destruction. This is how we attach ourselves to the *old* story and keep repeating it. This is how we attack others and make them responsible for our misfortune. The pain is so deep, but the intentions are so good, so loving. How could there be fault there? How could you blame others, and at the same time exonerate yourself in the name of love?

This conflict became clearer and clearer. One of the two ends were faulty. Either the *pain* is real or the *love* is real. Either the pain is real and someone else is inflicting that pain, and if that is the case, how can I love them? Or the love is real, I love them from a place of abundance, and if that is the case, how can they hurt me?

The breakthrough which unlocked this conundrum was something I learned from ***A Course in Miracles*** by Helen Schucman.

Nothing real can be threatened. Nothing unreal exists. Herein lies the peace of God.
~ *A Course in Miracles*

If, in fact, nothing *unreal* exists, then what exists is *real*. Both pain and love must then be real. They can be felt in our skin. They both materialize in actions. Even feelings exist and become real in the physical realm.

I then started accepting that both were real in their own essences. So, if they are both real, can they be threatened? Can real love be threatened? After what seemed a lifetime of back-and-forth dwelling on these ideas of feelings and reality, something came to heart:

Real love cannot be threatened, but love that comes from *fear* certainly can.

Yes. It's hard to find out that what you thought to be love really isn't. It is shameful and disappointing to come to the realization that all the love you believed you were giving is fake love.

To avoid the idea that we have been unloving, we would do anything. Even if it is repeating the pattern, hoping that that fake love will turn into real love all by itself. Can you imagine the anxiety this would create in a human being with a divine soul?

So, yes. Unloving.

I can say today that I was terrified not to be loved back, so I loved from fear. And the love I gave to others, even if it had amazing intentions, was a fake love. There. I'm okay with it. I'm loving it. I love and accept the scared little girl looking for love and acceptance. I don't want to shut her up, I don't want to convict her with a death sentence.

I simply want to love her.

Women, this is the little girl you will never be able to get rid of. No one can. On occasion, it will feel like a little *monster* with bones and flesh and with the raw irrational feelings that come with it. And it is okay. We are allowed to experience this state of *scarcity* as humans. And thank God for that! This experience of scarcity and pain is what sparks our soul to start a journey in search of something higher.

Women, this is the little girl we sometimes want our partner to hold and embrace. And it is so frustrating when they don't, right? Women, trust me, love your little girl because the more love you give to her, the sweeter she will become. Every man loves a sweet little girl loved by an authentic woman.

This book is not to show you the light at the end of the tunnel. Or much less to tell you about it! I know you know the light is there! This book is to turn your eyes to the center of your heart, so you can see a very incipient reflection of that light within yourself. For you would never be able to recognize that light outside of you if you didn't have a pretty amazing abundant light within.

Retelling the old story of who you were keeps you away from your path of light and realization. It sets you back into blame-land. To shine your light, you must love your darkness and thank it.

Thank it all. Make amends with the past and let it go.

Affirmations of Power

I love and appreciate the side of me that desperately *cries* for love and acceptance.

I release who I have been up to today and am ready to uncover my true *identity*.

I *forgive* myself for the pain that I have inflicted on others while searching for my true self.

Finding the *Real* You in There

We attach ourselves to our past because we have mistaken it for our *identity*.

We often see who we are as what we have done, or what we have missed doing. What we have been able to accomplish or not. We see an image of ourselves that our mind has created and then hate it, attack it, despise it within ourselves. Then we present it to others in the nicest way for it to be loved and accepted. If it's then loved and validated from an external source, we hope to feel finally loved, relaxed, and free of fear.

You might not agree with this, but we are loved by others more often than not. Most people are seeking affection by pleasing others. Trust me, being loved and accepted by others can be pretty easy. Yet, we still don't feel truly loved. We still feel no satisfaction deep in our soul, and we hunger for more. Then, we believe we need more acceptance. So we start disclosing more about our story, our path, what we have done, what we want to do. We do this to elicit more acceptance and relevance in other people's eyes. Then again, we enjoy their praise like the most delicious dessert. This pleasure dissipates soon after, and leaves us again in a state of desperation.

This desperation, if you have felt it before, is not desperation that makes you cry long and hard. It's desperation in disguise. It often makes its entrance as feelings of wanting to connect and deeply love and feel loved by someone else. Someone who doesn't know the side of us we so much despise.

Often, in this situation, people find the urge to start anew. Start from scratch. Go somewhere where no one knows them, where they can erase their past. If you are trying to erase your behavior so you do not have to look at it again, please give up on feeling loved by others for the rest of your life. You will not allow yourself the pleasure of receiving that gift, for they don't know who they are with, or so you think. Even if they love you for who you are and not what you have done, you do not love yourself in the same way. How can we then feel loved if we don't fully love ourselves?

Words of Wisdom

Easier said than done. Most of us oscillate between wanting to be open and truthful and wanting to hide just this little piece that is after all, oh-so-irrelevant.

Until you are receiving the most wanted hug from someone you care about, and then a shameful thought about yourself enters your head. Between the fight of your mind and your heart to decide if you are worthy of the hug, the moment is over. You oscillated between the past and future at such a high frequency you fell astray from the present.

The same way we sometimes come clean with someone else, we should come clean with ourselves. In such a way that makes us see and understand the struggle the other part of us is experiencing on a daily basis.

Do not despise that other person inside and judge it like you judge others! Someone said: The way you judge others is the same way you will be judged. We do not have to go too far to find someone who would judge us that way. It is ourselves. And as a matter of fact, that's why we judge others in the first place. Because that is the way we treat ourselves.

I wonder then, if we judge others harshly because we do the same to ourselves. Can we love others if we do not fully love and accept ourselves?

We have heard so many phrases like, *love yourself before you love others* in so many ways, shapes, and shades. But how do we do that? It's not a button we have hidden somewhere that we can push that will naturally awaken a dormant part of us. It is not as simple as executing a command, and voila, we suddenly love ourselves.

It's not a button, but wait, could it be?

A button is a trigger that kicks off one or a series of commands to be executed. In the case of self-love, the button is the decision you make, it's the trigger, the desire and the belief you need to love yourself. This puts in motion the commands to achieve what you want.

But wait, how many times have we flipped that switch? How many times have we pressed that button? Tomorrow I start loving myself. Or wait, I love myself now. Yet it hasn't worked.

You still *expect*. You still expect others to accept you so you can truly love yourself. And I'm talking about higher love here.

I mean loving yourself at such a degree, deeply and profoundly, that you can love others from your true identity. Not the shade your identity has created, guided by your mind. I'm talking a love from which you can share with others your identity guided by your heart.

So, we have been pressing that button, the *self-love-now* button, and nothing comes out. Nothing new happens. Empty. Zero. It says *self-love-now,* seems right. But what is going on? I press this button and I'm just doing more of the same!

What if we are pressing the right button but in the wrong place? What if we have been hitting the self-love button from the mind and not the heart? Wait, could it be that the self-love button from the heart might yield different instructions?

Wow, I didn't know about this heart-mind thing. This is fascinating! You mean to tell me if I hit the self-love button from the heart, I will find the real instructions that would allow me to love and accept myself fully?

Well, yes. That is what I'm suggesting you do. Stop hitting the mind and asking it to do things it doesn't know how to do. This love thing is not a trade, it's not a scientific measurable thing we can quantify, plan or ration. The ways of the mind won't work for the things outside of its domain. And love; it is certainly from the heart.

So, what will happen if we decide to press the self-love button from the heart? First thing, the mind freaks out, like yours might be doing right at this second. It identifies all of these well-justified reasons why that's a bad idea. And why? Well, see, the mind is not only currently in control of your self-love, but of so many other things. You will find the mind is responsible for so much other heart stuff. If we could find those other things and return them to their true owner, we would experience a sense of relaxation and balance.

The real you in there is an amazing human being and a divine soul. There is nothing wrong with you, or me, I discovered. We are perfectly created, we just have a few glitches to tune up. There are a few responsibilities that need to be reassigned, a few rules to re-write, and that's all.

Think about it, we are so lucky that's the case. Animals and simple-minded humans live happily for the most part, but they do not *fully* know they are happy. They are not aware of the blessing of the journey to happiness.

But the mind freaks. That's what it does, and it does it well. That's its job, after all. The mind was created for survival, for reactive instincts. Do you know why it feels threatened when it comes to things of the heart?

Because to the mind, the heart's algorithm to love is not reliable. The mind is guided by a set of ideas and rules it believes will take us to a safe place where we can avoid pain.

The mind strives for *security,* not *fulfillment.*

This primitive system of the mind was installed on purpose. It's okay if the mind freaks. Watch it freak. Become aware and stand in your *duality.* The mind sees imminent death, because if you take away one of the things it controls, it messes up the rules for all else. Imagine that! If you take away love from the mind, what would happen to happiness? The mind also has a few rules for happiness that are messing you up, preventing you from reaching the top of the very feeling it controls.

You will never be able to turn off the mind's fear of death. It will always be present in your physical reality. And you can't live your daily life in an alpha-state either. So, what's left?

Dealing with it.

Let's make peace with that first. After all, perfection is so boring! It would mean someone would love you for being perfect and not for who you are. Acknowledging your *human* mind, making mistakes, makes us feel the love in a whole new way. We are not perfect, yet we are loved. So embrace your imperfection, your human mind, and let's deal with it.

What's the biggest fear of the mind?

The mind's biggest fear is that if you rearrange the way it's been wired to find love and worthiness, it will mess up the algorithm and it will *never* get it.

The mind thinks that pushing through with the current algorithm will lead to love someday. Do you see? That's why, in the first place, we can't get rid of our minds.

The mind is working for the *same* purpose as the heart. That purpose is *love*.

Yet, the mind and the heart arrive at love through different means. You hear many people say when referring to a harsh person: He or she doesn't have a heart. And what do they mean? Obviously, the person does have a literal heart or he wouldn't be walking down the sidewalk. Instead, they mean: Look, that person is not behaving from his or her heart. That person is trying to achieve a loving purpose through *not-loving* means. Ah! And why? Why would a loving person attempt to emotionally or physically hurt another human being in the name of love?

I know this might be a delicate question. Many of you reading this might believe you are or have been a victim of abuse. For the purpose of the self-love topic we are discussing, I want to say that a human will often react from their survival instinct when it fears death.

To that person trying to receive or feel love, it's a matter of life *and* death. They do not know any other means of obtaining the love they crave, and when those means are shut down, there is no way out for them. At that instant, it's either you or their survival. For they will die if they cannot experience the feeling they are so desperately seeking.

They are unable to generate such love for themselves. They are on the lookout for the person who will take the responsibility of their emotions and will give them unconditional love.

This might give you a hint of why, if this is your case, you have attracted people who lack self-love to your life. You probably do not love yourself either. You are probably also looking for your love to be satisfied and validated first from an external source. You are waiting for someone to label you as lovable, so then you can relax, accept, and love yourself.

The mind is absolutely certain that if it lets go, the hope to feel the love it desperately needs will vanish.

Most of the time we ask the mind to step away. We tell it that it doesn't know how to love, we blame it for having made the wrong decisions in the past, and we just want to get rid of it. Can you imagine what it would be like to tell God to stop loving you? Well, this is similar.

Try telling your mind to stop protecting you. Instead, what if we approach our minds differently? What if you pamper it, give it security, comfort? What if you tell that unloved part of yourself that it doesn't need to search for its survival out there? What if we tell that desperate unloved us that we accept its nature? What if we thank the mind for all the times it took on the job of the lazy heart, even when it didn't know how?

After all, it held the fort for so long. It held you up while you were figuring out that thing called *awareness*.

It protected you from your first heartbreak. It shielded you from those horrible comments you once heard about yourself. The mind had no choice but to react the way it did. It installed those old decrees that scrambled your values and their rules. Your heart was not mature enough to respond back then. But your mind did. Someone had to! And guess what? It did its job. And did it well.

Feel blessed.

It's time to understand how blessed we are. Look around. Look at the immense energy that has emanated from the universe, others, and yourself, to be here right now. You are at the threshold of your real-self, which is, after all, pure unconditional love.

Today you meet your *vulnerable* self without feeling *sorry* for it.

Today, you realize your mind was never damaged, but it has taken care of you. Today, you realize you have been guided and protected from your own internal wisdom. And today is the day that wisdom has been given back to you, intact and ready to recover your true natural state of communion with yourself.

Today, you realize that feelings of blame and shame for yourself have no room in your new understanding of the universe and its purpose.

All souls *must* return home.
You are on your way *back*.

Can you start to notice how amazing it feels? No shame, no blame. No anxiety to be singled out, no fear of being guilty. Just an absolute understanding of the purpose of your journey. An absolute certainty of how blessed each and every one of us are.

If tears flow down your face, that's okay. My tears are flowing, too. Maybe some images from the past will pop into your mind. Your mind jumps to rewrite them, very quickly, to again protect you and keep you from any further pain. Do you understand the mind a little better now?

But before the mind has a chance, your heart steps in and says:

I love you,

I'm sorry,

Please forgive me,

Thank you,

I love you,

I'm sorry,

Please forgive me,

Thank you,

I love you,

I'm sorry,

Please forgive me,

Thank you.

Your beautiful mind steps away as the last tear runs down your face. It has fulfilled its mission. It has delivered you safe and sound to your heart. You made it. Your mind can rest now. It can go take care of the survival stuff, and grow in its own wisdom. As a result, you will live a much healthier life. You will not dwell in damaging emotions that deteriorate you physically. Your anxiety will disappear.

You might have stressful *moments,* but not a stressful *life.* A moment of *doubt,* but not a life of *insecurity.*

This is who you really are. Your heart in full bloom. Not the collection of your actions under a survival blueprint. You are the good faith of your intentions aligned with an intelligent plan for greatness.

Affirmations of Power

I'm a higher being with an infinite set of gifts and powers.

I can and will find myself.

My mind gladly steps aside so my heart can take control of my destiny.

STEP TWO

Forgiving What You Did and Not Who You Are

~ And I lived through the day I faced my darkest side to find a bloom at the other side. ~

We have all had a glance of the real us several times in our lives. In fact, we know ourselves and our full potential deep inside. And we truly know how to uncover that better human we aspire to be.

Yet we do not do it. It takes a lot of ourselves to make a real change, a transformation that is effective and that lasts.

It is critical we learn how to make the real us more permanent. It is crucial we find a way to make the true us stick around for longer once we finally manage to uncover it.

Now that we know that divine human is in there, and once we have felt its drive and its power, we will dive a little deeper into what it takes to forgive ourselves truly.

I know this might sound just like another "forgive yourself" fluff statement to you. A shallow state where we just go back to those moments and revise them one by one trying to find one we can truly forgive. Yet we come out the other side exactly the same, if not worse. Hurting by having re-lived those memories without a clearer perspective.

What we are going to do is different. We are not going to forgive our past actions or decisions by minimizing them, but by looking at them differently. I want us to see and understand the human being who did not know better back then, the human who was hurting.

We will see ourselves for who we really are, so that we can walk steady and strong a little further into our path to realization.

The Difference Between *Behavior* and *Identity*

I have been my worst enemy.

The idea of blaming others feels so old now. Every person I have ever blamed in my life was an instant victim of my own frustrations and limitations. No one has treated me worse than I have treated myself.

The idea that my partner hurt me is debatable. I let myself be hurt. His offensive words and painful actions emotionally confirmed over and over the mistreatment I was offering myself. It is true another person would not have behaved the same way. But it is also true I wouldn't have gotten this incredible chance for massive transformation.

No one abused me more than I did. In that way, I'm my own abuser. Those who walk through life hurting others are at the edge of emotional death. They are on the verge of not feeling their real selves ever again if they don't act quickly. Forgive them.

What saved me was my deep desire for healing. My emphatic and self-unloving nature was the combination that attracted takers in my life. I needed those experiences to wake up as I was becoming a taker myself. It was the ultimate test.

Either you *overcome* it,
or you *become* it.

Who do you choose to be? That's the moment you find out what you are really made of. Whether you take the pain and push through or you succumb to the lesson's polarity.

That's when your true identity shows up.

That's when you might behave completely differently than you have ever behaved. That's when the shadow has no choice but to step aside and let the light shine through you.

Words of Wisdom

How we react to a stimulus, either physical or emotional, speaks to our behavior—how we conduct ourselves toward others. We often judge others according to their behavior. *He never says good morning*—he is "antisocial." *She is always flirting with men*— she is an "easy woman." It is very hard for our minds not to judge every interaction, every conversation.

This silent collection of automatic thoughts and those judgmental ideas are up for grabs when we need to use them. They are easy to retrieve and the mind does not hesitate to access them to protect itself from what it believes to be detrimental emotional damage.

It is very hard to change the fact we judge ourselves and others. But it is even harder to live with the belief that we are what we think of ourselves.

This is a powerful thought. Think about it. What if we are not what we think we are? What if the image you have of yourself and that you judge silently and unconsciously day and night is not you?

I know you have thought about this, and heard this liberating idea before. You might have even given it some thought, gone into meditation or had a dream. You might have forgiven yourself already for your own past many times. But, somehow, this silent judgment is still there. It comes back. It haunts you in nights of solitude.

I have thought about this deep and hard. And I realized that maybe the reason we cannot let go of those judgments is the belief that someone must have inflicted the pain. Who is going to be responsible for the old you? How can you explain that you have behaved in a certain way up to today, and that is just simply not you? While the idea sounds pretty damn liberating, can we just let that go with no explanation?

The mind has trouble with magic. The mind needs a logical explanation. And in this case, there is.

You are not who you have been up to today. You are you, plus a belief system, an array of values and rules that wired you to behave and act the way you have up until today. You have a history, an upbringing, a programming. That, installed on top of yourself, has resulted in the person who lived up to today.

Your behavior is not your identity.
~ Tony Robbins

Your past actions are the clothes you wore. Your actions today are what you are wearing. Yes. Some opt to live with the same wardrobe their whole lives. But most of them never knew they could change them. And some never even knew they were wearing clothes. You can change your clothes. It would be hard to get a new body, but you can change what you wear.

It is extremely difficult to change your heart's feelings about something. But if you change your perception of it, the way you interpret that something, you will feel different about it.

You are your *heart*.

Your identity. It runs deeper than your thoughts and your mind. You can change your ideas, your reasoning. It will automatically translate in a change of vision, understanding, and ultimately, feeling. Thus, changing a behavior by conditioning can be a painful process. But changing yourself by changing the model of your world will result in an automatic desirable result.

It's hard to change yourself, but it is easy to change your patterns, thoughts, and the programming you have been living with.

You are free. You can keep the clothes you like, and discard the rest. You are not tied to your behaviors and your thoughts. Even if it feels like they are glued to you right now.

Give this crazy thought a thought.

What if you could detach them from you?

Affirmations of Power

I *forgive* myself.

I'm *blessed* and *guided* in
every moment of my life.

Every time I close my eyes, I have
the power to *reclaim* my *true* identity.

The Things the *Monster* Has Done

Detaching from the consequences of our past, and the present our old decisions have created, hurts like hell. Most people want to change and are ready to heal. They dream of moving on from a certain situation, but what stops them might not be the past itself, but their present—what their lives look like at the present moment when they want to change the most.

And that is how the universe works, isn't it? It wouldn't be a test otherwise, would it? How could we prove to ourselves that we have healed, that we are able to forgive ourselves and others, and make better decisions?

I have ended a family for the second time, after seven years of horror. I came in and stayed in this unhealthy relationship, desperate to feel the love I did not know how to give myself. I was running from the healing I needed several years ago and chose to hide from the pain I still have to face today. Doubled.

Now I have to face the pain of seeing my children leave home for long hours. I have to feel the excruciating pain of knowing I will not enjoy the family of my dreams. God knows how much I wanted to parent together with the father of my babies. Yet I was a slave to myself. And I entered a painful and destructive relationship that brought me every single lesson I needed to snap out of this pattern. And ultimately, it taught me to how to love myself.

To get that result, you need a person who is able to deliver that kind of lesson. Because hurtful people do not love themselves, they spend their lives trying to get the love they're missing inside from someone else. Some elicit that love by inflicting pain on others. Others elicit the same love by being extremely pleasing and giving. Codependents, for example, do it by venerating and giving excessively to the other person, allowing and enabling the damaging behaviors of their partners.

I made myself responsible for someone else's journey without realizing that what I'm responsible for is my own journey, my own feelings, my own life. I was dependent on my partner to tell me I was a kind person for me to feel as such. I craved his gratitude so I could feel needed and loved. I relied on him to make me believe these things, so I became dependent on him.

I snapped out of codependency and met myself. I started the journey back to self-love, acceptance and fulfillment. But it is difficult. My present is a perfect drawing of my old life.

The idea I'm explaining here is how hard can it be to move forward, even when you know the way, under the consequences of your life until today.

Words of Wisdom

Drawing a line between your new and *old* self could be frightening. After all, all the *love* you have experienced until now was by being your old self. But remember all the *pain*, too. This is hard to remember, because it is easier for the human being to *receive*—even if it's not something so good—than to *lack*.

Think about this for a minute. Sometimes we don't pay as much attention to what we receive as long as we are *receiving something*. This is a huge signal of lack of self-love.

When we give up our own desires, bend our own values and rules to get a deeper need met, we bend ourselves over to get the feeling we seek.

Later, we realize that when we pursue our destiny *sacrificing* our own identity, there is no *fulfillment*. We are unable to feel loved and accepted. Consider this: who was pursuing the feeling after all? It wasn't you. It was the version of you that you created to be able to achieve the purpose.

Telling yourself this old being is done functioning is a terrifying step. Also, because that being might have gotten used to eliciting love out of his own mistakes and shortcomings. If you were to not be your old self any longer, you would have to not only come up with a new way to *avoid* pain but also a new way to *elicit* love.

This is the way the old you thinks and reasons. Notice. The old you thinks life is about avoiding pain and eliciting love. What we are going to discover is that the *new you* knows something quite different. A little, sacred secret of the old masters.

In the presence of *real* love, there is no *pain*.

Instead, life is about finding and igniting that source of abundance. That source is within us. Tapping into that energy will open your heart to channel a love that is so immense, that is not created but rather *transformed* and *shared*.

Real love is never found outside of ourselves.

Your *old self* thinks you are not worthy of that kind of love. After all, look at what you have done up to today. How much you have lost, how much you have missed. Your actions and inactions. The things you have said, your regrets, your past. The *old* story surfaces to remind you of the damage. On top of it all, it looks at how much work you have to put in to keep up this *new self* long enough for others to believe it and accept it.

Notice.

Again.

Your old self wants you to believe the new you will also look for approval and love in others first. That is the story it needs to keep up so you resign from this quest. How would the people from your past love and accept the *new you*, after all?

A real transformation will
never be for others, *initially*.

It happens from a deep realization that you will never reach your fulfillment from a state of *self-pity* or *self-hate*.

The past is your teacher. If you want to take this journey, embrace it. Talk about it from the perspective of learning. Do something *beautiful* with the pain of the past. These experiences were given to you as gifts.

Your biggest problem is that you
think you shouldn't have problems.
~ Tony Robbins

If I hadn't gone through the deepest *pain* of not loving myself, I would never have written this book. If I hadn't been bold enough to express my darkest feelings and thoughts of misery in front of 5,000 other human beings, I would never have received the gift of real love.

The day I felt the deepest love in my soul was the day I showed myself to the world as an *unloving* creature. That day, after despising myself for hours, I finally gave in to who I *was*. I accepted my humanness and the *role* of pain in my life. Since that time, I've wondered, how could that moment be a blessing instead of a nightmare? I asked myself a question that *Tony Robbins* embedded in our new selves: How could life be happening *for* me and not *to* me?

Life happens for you, not to you.
~ Tony Robbins

Right in that second, I looked up to the sky, my face covered in tears, and I said I didn't understand it then, but I knew that deep within, a bigger purpose was beginning to take shape. It had to. My soul was ripped open. I could feel the flesh of my heart stretching, reorganizing. I was feeling *loved* for the first time, from strangers. And I cried, so hard. For I had never loved myself before like they were loving me.

I then experienced a feeling I never had experienced before. *I met* myself. Somewhere in the middle of my old and new self. I met the true *essence* of my soul.

Your past is your key to your self-mirror. Dress up with all your past and be loved by it.

You are totally *worth* it!

Affirmations of Power

I'm not my *past*.

I can redefine my life
by redefining *myself*.

I accept who I behaved as, so
I can embrace my true *identity*.

Making Peace With the *Monster*

I noticed multiple times in my life I had decided to change. Change *this*, change *that*. I remember so many moments in which I carefully designed what I wanted to tweak about me. I worked hard to get to a version of myself that was more acceptable to others. Oh, and that somehow didn't totally violate my principles.

Wow. What is wrong with that?

Now I feel I have *changed* in a different way. Because it is not an orchestrated change in the name of pitifully eliciting from others what I didn't know I was lacking. It's the change that happens when you meet yourself and decide to say *YES* to discovering who you truly are.

I faced the question and have decided to jump off the cliff of *security* and *significance*. In this exploring of myself, I'm ready to accept that I do not know what I look like in my *own* mirror, and cannot project an image I can predict could be acceptable to others.

Enough of that *slavery*.

This pattern was so hidden to my eyes. I could not see it. I could feel it, but I could not understand it and grasp the danger it represented to myself and those around me.

I do wonder sometimes what could have happened if I had healed sooner. But I now understand that is a question that belongs to the *old* pattern.

After all, I'm healed now.

I'm alive, healed and centered. Yet that is something I needed to do without expectations of how others would react to the *real* me. They are in their own path. I ceased to be a source of narcissistic supply by stopping my pattern. But that does not guarantee the cessation of theirs. It could lead to their healing, or onto another source that is where I was a couple of months ago.

He will do *her* a favor by presenting the lessons she needs to ultimately love herself. And *she* will give him the chance to snap out of his own narcissistic approach and take a chance at *real* love. Again. In any case, they are the perfect *painful* match until one of them joins the land of the *free,* by choice.

Words of Wisdom

What's done is done. What you did and what was done to you. Today, maybe you want to take a different approach and consider it was not something that just happened to you but for you.

Yes. Maybe.

Would you be here otherwise? How much did it take to get you here on the verge of yourself? How much energy and how much effort from so many people in your life to shape your destiny up to this point?

That's why sometimes I just say: yes, thank you. When I remember what I've been through and all those generous souls that were willing to intercept my *singular* destiny to help me fulfill my purpose. And theirs.

Don't get me wrong. The universe is economic. Trust me on this. The same way we are fulfilling ours, they are fulfilling theirs and we are a chess pieces in their game.

Life is that beautiful, as unexpected, as totally carefully designed. For everyone's benefit and everyone's lessons. Hard and sweet. Forgiving and challenging.

Life is that. A collection of lessons carefully planned out. Chosen by us.

What happened was necessary. Most of the times we have serious trouble moving forward because of the past damage. Damage to ourselves and to others.

That's okay.

Look. Most of us humans don't even get to merge our own story with our true selves. Ever. We finish this earthly passage and we returned *unnamed*. Only the *soul* will prevail.

What could be sadder than that? Than not realizing while we are alive that we have met, or at least tried, to meet our purpose?

So, there you have it. Two choices. Face your past, which is not so dark, trust me. And walk toward the light of self-contemplation. Or hide from it. Until you can. And never explore your real self further.

If you have read this far, you have probably decided to face your *wins* and your *loses*. Wise soul. For you will enter now a whole new realm of understanding and perception.

From the *acceptance* of your past
comes the willingness to *embrace*
the *uncertainty* of your future.

This is so beautiful. It means you now trust and believe in a whole new part of yourself to deliver your satisfaction and fulfillment.

The quality of your life is directly
proportional to the amount of
uncertainty you can live with.
~ Tony Robbins

It took me a long time to make peace with myself. Now that I look back, I ask what the most difficult feature to accept was. What was the feature I would work the hardest to hide from others and mostly myself?

It was the fact I couldn't feel the love from others. I wasn't able to feel loved like I somehow craved to feel. I worked hard to hide that fact. I could only think about the disappointment and frustration of those around me if I expressed I wasn't able to feel loved by them despite their efforts. I knew it somehow had to do with me. I just couldn't put my finger on how.

Carrying this feeling got pretty heavy. It created an internal separation from those who were closer to me. Despite my intention to connect, to merge, to become one, it didn't happen. I always thought I was approaching it the right way.

I realized afterward that my approach was pleasing and unloving at the same time. Giving love became a ritual of artificial pleasing. Hoping for the other person to feel loved and satisfied first. So that then they could love me in a way that could fill me, and I could finally feel it.

I look back now, and I can barely believe this was my life. That I actually lived with this attachment pattern for so long. Two marriages, three children and so many years of well-intentioned, open-hearted attempts based on faulty software.

It took a lot to get here. I find peace right in this second when I realize I actually made it here. That I'm on the other side of that millenary journey of the quest for myself.

It's peaceful here.

It will be peaceful on the other side of your journey, as well.

You are worth whatever it takes to get there. Meeting your core will give back to yourself and those around you in a way you cannot possibly measure. It can't be quantified in terms of love. But it will for sure make your life more productive. You will reach and surpass your goals and expectations. Naturally.

That's why you should consider letting go. Asking the mind to step away for a while from your past and what has happened to the old you. At least until you can advance far enough down the line to then see your past in a different light.

Letting go can be very easy or it can be very hard. It depends on the result you ultimately want. Dare to undress from your past. There will still be you. A you who can think and feel more responsibly. It is authentic, and it is aligned with your heart. This you will take you far.

Give it a chance.

Affirmations of Power

I *forgive* myself for the past decisions that *separated* me from my *true* self.

I'm *grateful* for the service of those who have intercepted my path.

I let go of my past *behavior* and understand what served me then does not serve the *new* model of my world.

What Your Identity *Truly* Is

We all know who we are deep inside or there wouldn't be any conflicts. The battle between our dualities has to do precisely with the absolute certainty that we know who we truly are. Even if we cannot manifest it, even if we cannot act from that heavenly place of center. We know we have felt it before, and we inevitably feel an urge to return to that center.

It is the center of our own balance of mind and heart. A place that knows how to act rather than react. It executes *heart-centered* thoughts.

Mind and heart aligned.

We have experienced that feeling somewhere and at some point before in our millenary existence.

It is within us.

We know who we are.

I remember the day I became aware of my soul in this lifetime. I was around six years old. It was a rainy morning, and for some reason, I couldn't bring myself to play as I would normally. I was uneasy as if something was wanting to come out of me. A realization was brewing, a feeling I myself could not understand at such an early age. I fought it until I decided to surrender and just experience it.

I remember thinking that the feeling wanted me to sing out loud about some sort of God, a *heavenly* being. It wanted me to express gratitude and sing out loud the feelings it was awakening in me. I recall it filling my heart with light and wisdom. I was just six years old! I had no idea what was happening to me. I had no idea where the words coming out of my mouth were coming from.

But the feeling was so genuine I decided to let it sing through me and make the sounds it wanted to make. I remember feeling embarrassed, singing a song that didn't even exist. Out loud! About a God I hadn't even been taught about before. It certainly wasn't the god I heard my grandmother speak about. The punishing god. It was another force totally pure, forgiving and benevolent. A force beyond any reasoning or judgment.

So, I let it be. I started crying as the words and melody came out of my mouth. I laid down in my bed and placed my feet against the wall, looking up to the ceiling. There was a painting on the wall. It was a picture of a wide-open field of beautiful, green grass and small bushes. Later in life, I heard someone say my name meant wide-open prairie. Maybe I was singing to myself. Maybe I was creating an anchor I could unconsciously go back to in moments of despair and disbelief.

That moment I knew there was something bigger out there that identified with something I carried inside. That day I realized that I had a piece of that beauty within me. I also discovered I could turn it on every time I closed my eyes and saw myself standing in a green field of peaceful, infinite grass.

I do that often. Actually, every time I go into a meditative state. I first go and sit in a crisscross position in the prairie. And there I relax and wait to be picked up by the masters who take me to the worlds of the unknown.

That feeling is so deep within me, it never allowed me to completely lose myself. It kept me whole even when I allowed others to shake my world.

I was *shaking* but I never
forgot I was *unshakable*.

Words of Wisdom

Our identity was meant to be silent for this long. The values and rules you have been living by are, in essence, a defense mechanism you have created to shield your heart from damage. Damage you believed existed. Damage which is an illusion of the mind's primary source of energy: *fear*.

We became unaware of our own divinity so we could have the opportunity to pave our way to self-awareness. Now that you are here, and you are becoming aware of not being aware of your true identity, can you remember a point in your life when you felt your soul at its fullest?

Go back to that moment, live it, amplify it, experience it. What did you feel then? How did you breathe? How open was your heart to these feelings? Now, try to remember the first instant right after this experience. How did you talk yourself out of this divinity state?

That is, in a nutshell, your programming. What did you say to yourself to come out of this state? When your mind kicked in, what did it tell you?

The exact words are not that important. What's relevant is the fact that you now know the mind came in to meddle and protect the vulnerability of your heart in that moment. And it reinforced your need for protection.

The *limit* is always the *mind*.

Consider you are going on your daily run, which is five miles. You are now comfortable running five miles every day. There is going to be one day you will go past five and run some more. You will feel strong, amazing, and you will keep going until suddenly, you realize you are past the regular five miles, and you actually feel great, you can do more.

But what usually happens? The mind attempts to tell you you are a five-miler. You start looking for what could go wrong or become anxious thinking if you go over five miles today, now every day you will need to deliver the new standard.

If you get in your head, you are dead.
~ Tony Robbins

Exactly the same happens when the heart stretches for growth. The mind freaks out. It is its job to do so. And it is okay. We have been told somehow that we have a bad mind that interferes in processes and mixes and misinterprets things.

Understanding the job of the mind frees you from being a slave to its reactions.

The mind will freak out for a moment, and that is okay. That is the voice of the mind. Just make sure your heart also gets a say. Let the heart also do its job. You need both, in harmony. If you are a heart with no mind or a mind with no heart, and you eliminate the conflict, you also eliminate the beauty and the magic that comes from the perfect dance between the two.

The *equilibrium* is where happiness is.

Now you know you never stopped being who you really are. You have always been whole. That internal knowledge is what has brought you back to the threshold of your own divine self.

Embrace it.

Affirmations of Power

I'm *whole* and *complete* as the universe purposely created me to be.

My *mind* is the horse, but my *heart* is the coachman.

My soul is *unshakable*.

STEP THREE

Seeing Others for Who They Are and Not What They Have Done

~ Touch their hearts, not their minds. ~

Making peace with ourselves, our past, and accepting our present was hard enough. Yet, we have not won the war yet. We have a battle under our belts, but there are a few more steps we must take if we want to put real love into practice.

Exonerating and forgiving ourselves truly wouldn't be sincere and complete without taking a moment to see others in the same way we see ourselves, and the role that their pain and their sacrifice have had in our lives.

When we make peace with ourselves, we enter a whole new world of possibilities, but truly forgiving others and seeing them for who they really are is what populates that new world we now live in.

Suddenly we see others in a whole new way, and possibilities arise. Suddenly relationships are possible, friends and coworkers are easier to interact with. What you will find out as you continue through this journey is that as you treat yourself better, and as you are kind to yourself, you will serve others better as well. Let's take a moment to revise our past with this new lens.

There Was *Really* No Damage

I'm getting divorced for the second time. I have three beautiful, loving children, yet I will never get to share a home with their father.

The first time I married I was so certain I would be married for life. I flaunted my marriage, saying I would never be a divorced woman. I took the perfect portraits at the perfect vacations. Vacations I would put together by myself. I would sell the perfect idea of the experience I wanted to my husband every time, hoping he would say yes when he found out it was all planned out in my head and ready to be executed.

I had the perfect husband. He would say yes, we would get the vacation, take the perfect portrait, and have a good time. As expected. Then we would come back home.

Back. Home. And not moving forward somewhere out there in the wilderness of life.

There was not much growth and progress. I played that game with myself until somewhere my unconscious got the message. At that pace, higher goals were going to have to wait until the next round on Earth.

I loved him, according to my childish concept of love back then, but I didn't love myself. I was lost in my desperate search for fulfillment, which I believed was somewhere else. I was determined to go there and grab it.

I was born with this very pronounced drive to search for a higher truth. Nothing in my life has been stronger than this. Not the very principles I was raised under. Not society's rules. Not the rules for marriage or divorce. Nothing. Not even my own life. For I believe the purpose of life itself is to attain the highest truth I can possibly reach.

I actually believed at some point I had suffered. And I probably did back then. But I do not suffer now for past sufferings.

Pain, like *time,* is relative to our awareness.

It hurt so much, though. It felt so real. My pain, and how others were vehicles of that pain. How much they inflicted this pain on me. Over and over again.

Yet, a part of me actually believes there is no damage. Am I crazy? How is that possible? What insane part of me can make peace with this? Why am I not shaking, losing control, depressed? How can I be full of life, raising my children and having an understanding of life?

Words of Wisdom

In a state of ***abundance***, nothing is missing. Everything is at peace. Still.

Scarcity brings on a different game. Scarcity means some have, and others lack. Those who lack want to have, and they want to move toward having. This is the story of development and evolution. A way to create emotional *scarcity* and *lacking* is to believe there has been damage caused by the pain and the lack of self-awareness of others.

Perceiving damage in the actions of others is a necessary illusion. It is necessary to create the scarcity to start the movement toward evolution and change.

If you hadn't been presented with what you don't want to feel, or with what hurts, how would you know what *not* to be? If you hadn't been wronged, how could you ever have the opportunity not to wrong back? Maybe to make a conscious choice, we need to be presented with its counterpart.

So, what if, in life, we take a different approach to the difficult times?

> What if your worst day was your best day?
>
> ~ Tony Robbins

What if the darkest moment of your life was brought to you to make you strong? To make you shape yourself into who you needed to be to fulfill your purpose and mission? What if the biggest struggle of your life is the final push you needed to start your contribution journey?

Be joyous!

The universe does not invest this kind of energy if you are not ready. Trust the biggest process happening in your life. After all, how much control do you have of it, and of others? And how much happiness do you generate for yourself from controlling external circumstances? Sparks of satisfaction, but not lasting fulfillment?

Even when you feel certain, it is never for very long. It is always constrained to another circumstance you can't control. Either a period of time or the behavior and decisions others might make. What if you put your energy into emotional assets and not into liabilities? What if you switch to investing in your emotional state toward fulfillment? And not spending to just feel good?

When we spend, we take from one place and put in another. Think about it. To buy a meal, you deduct from your cash value and transfer the difference to the vendor. That money will not grow. It was an expense. You ate. Hours later you must eat again. It's a vital need, so you must spend to meet that need. If your resources are not replenished, you won't be able to cover that basic need to stay alive. You must replenish that source.

Then what happens to emotional and spiritual needs?

What is the *currency* for happiness?

Are we trading something for feelings? If we feel our emotional states are not whole and fulfilling, does it mean we engage ourselves in *debits* rather than *credits*?

Damage and pain come from a place of lacking and scarcity. Maybe we are taking resources out of one area and moving them to another one we believe would give us more pleasure. We then engage in this giant *whack-a-mole* game where every person involved has a hammer!

Like a mole, pain pops up in our lives rather unexpectedly. It shows up faster and faster, and we hit it again and again, trying to avoid it until we burst. We face pain with a huge hammer. It is the tool we have built to be able to survive it. We have been conditioned to respond this way. We see the mole showing up on our side as an *attack* and that's how we respond to it. We attack *back*.

What if we were to realize it is not about hitting them all, rather it's about realizing we are playing a never-ending game, and it's time to walk out?

What if we could choose again and realize we can survive "pain" by redefining it?

If you have walked out, or are considering doing so, please, take a moment to congratulate yourself. Watch the picture from the outside before you leave this place. Take a closer look. Look at those people's faces, holding onto their hammers for dear life. Feel for them. Thank them! For they hit the mole on their side that needed to come out on your side so you could realize it was an illusion.

Someone had to be *blind* so
you could *open* your *eyes*.

Thank them, for we are all players of our own destinies and agents of someone else's. Look at how angry they get when a mole pops up again on their side. See their reactions, how they label them as *problems*. Yet, one day you realized that problems were your biggest *blessings*. A signal from the heavens for you to snap out. Your own message in a bottle to *yourself*, delivered by a wave of *others*.

Oh, damage! So necessary, so painful . . . until one day we undress it and see the diamond within.

Oh! Before you go, remember that you will leave this circle. And you will move forward, there will be stops in life where you will see whack-a-mole tournaments all around you.

Players will tell you that you won't survive if you don't have a hammer. They will even hand you one! They will almost convince you they are doing you a favor and blame you for not wanting to hold on to one. They will tempt your mind to rebuild the self-protection mechanism that shields you from pain, but also from love.

They might call you names. They might attempt and even succeed at harming you. They might make you feel you are different than them because you are.

You are not better than them, you are just in a different stage of life and evolution.

It will be hard to walk and watch those games for a while. You will need to dwell in that middle ground until you do not need their validation and approval to move forward. Until you fully learn to love and appreciate yourself as a higher being.

Until you do not feel *tempted* to grab a hammer anymore, you will be offered one.

You will then be a different kind of *agent* in the lives of others. Still with a mission of helping others but from a contribution perspective; *dharmatic,* and not *karmatic.* Here is where we start to give back. Here is where the job ends and the mission starts.

One step closer to home.

Affirmations of Power

The path I'm *currently* on is carefully designed to help me fulfill my divine purpose.

What I *struggle* the most with in my life is precisely the next *lesson* I must decode.

My *healing* is the ultimate *purpose* of the *universe,* and life works in my favor.

The Amateur's Mistake

I received my first conscious awakening experience early in my adult life. I experienced an *out-of-body* sensation that slashed my fear of death.

It all started when I met a very dear person in my life. This encounter made me better understand the concept of soul companionship and purpose. We stumbled into each other in a hallway, and it felt like two energy waves had clashed. In some world, that clash produced noise. I could hear it.

We looked at each other confused, with a noble smile, as if we had met after a very long time. Millenniums. We both could tell that our souls recognized each other. Our spirits saluted. I could feel the honor, the bond. Something we both respected. As if we each had walked away from our bodies for the greeting. If you have been initiated in a mystical ancient order, you know what kind of connection I'm referring to. Soon we started getting closer to each other. We shared daily space, and it fostered our spiritual bond.

Our physical selves did not know how to handle that feeling. We mistook the feeling for a weird unexpected attraction we couldn't easily explain. Soon after, I was reading books and catching up to this spiritual world that I had re-discovered within. This was the start of the conscious journey back to myself.

Little did I know I was just starting!

As I began to walk down the path of conscious evolution, I made the most common mistake of enthusiastic beginners. I believed that, with a little bit of information, I knew everything about myself and others. I acted quickly by putting into practice what I believed I had learned.

I was so anxious to feel true love, identification, and connection that I desperately started looking at how to get there. I did not know I didn't love myself. I could not explain or notice my destructive anxiety and the effect it had on myself and others. I then found an explanation for my self-dissatisfaction: my life and the decisions I had made up until that day.

I then believed everyone else had a problem. That people who were not in the path weren't good enough, or smart enough, or evolved enough. I came to believe that was the source of my discontent. My relationships and not myself.

Well, you can tell by how this is going that I was setting myself up for the biggest lesson of them all: what makes a person spiritually advanced?

I made the huge mistake of flaunting my new discoveries and feeling better, higher, because of it. I put others down with comments, looks, and my behavior. I'm truly ashamed of it today, even though I see the grandiosity of the pain and the lessons to get me back to *myself,* finally.

I made the huge mistake of wanting to fix others and teach them. That's not the worst part. I did that while knowing deeply that there was nothing they could ever have done. Nothing could have worked for our relationships to work out. I was already too far ahead in my own head. Gone and derailed in the idea that I was, somehow, chosen, or special.

Life had a bigger plan to show me what spiritual development really was, after all.

And it did.

Words of Wisdom

We are the owners of our own destinies. That goes for building, but also for *destroying*. Why is it that you give yourself *credit* when you build, and *blame* others when you destroy? Is it possible it doesn't match the version of you or part of you you accept and love? If we must blame others for our misfortune and indulge in self-realization when we do make it, could it be that we are avoiding reflecting back to ourselves the part of us that needs to be loved the most? Are we our biggest enemy?

Think about that for a minute. When it comes to matters of the heart, we expect love from others but secretly despise ourselves.

It is from this position that we face the world of those around us. We pretend to *cure* them once we believe to have found the *formula* to heaven. We want them to *be* with us, because we know that if they *become,* we are then inclined to *do so* as well. We want to be us, but we do not know how to do so with *just* ourselves.

We want others to show us. So we push onto them what they might not be ready to consume just yet. And we do it in the name of love, understanding and compassion.

Growth is a very personal journey. The most precious moment in one's existence is the moment you internalize the answer to a question you have consciously asked yourself. That's when you realize the answer with your whole being, it merges with your conscious mind. It emerges from your unconscious and becomes now part of your aware self. This is your growth. A transfer from your hidden treasure chest to your hands, where you can see your own worth.

These gems do not come from anywhere else but yourself. This treasure you have inside of you, no one can take it away, just as you cannot take it from others. It has always been there. The more you can retrieve on this round on earth, the earlier you will be able to help others to discover their own worth, as well.

That moment in which you become aware that your best answers lie within is magical. It cannot be explained, reproduced or faked. Therefore, it cannot be precipitated onto others. If we give others answers to questions they haven't asked to themselves, their hearts will listen to your answer, but their minds won't be ready to process it and internalize it. Thus, generating suffering for others. Often pushing them away from the path. Often resenting the evolutionary journey they weren't ready for. At least, not yet.

Also, I invite you to review the purpose of why we would do such a thing. Try to fix others. We hope for others to read the book we read and get disappointed when they don't find the same amusement we did. It feels noble of us to want to share our lessons. But what's the real purpose behind that?

What's the real reason it bothers us to deal with someone who hasn't learned what we have learned? Could it be we cannot handle who we were before this change took place?

If this is the case, you have only worked half way. You discovered who you can be, but to be it fully, you must love and appreciate who you were, what you went through, for it brought you here.

So, is the lack of acceptance of others who are not at the same point in our path a sign that we do not accept and love ourselves? If we feel we have learned lessons and it's time to start brand new, with a clean slate, are we really facing and embracing the full spectrum of the magical process that spiritual growth is?

Anticipating growth in others, when they are not looking for it, is a way to delay their evolution. The person usually reacts to the imposed lesson with their minds, rather than their heart. They are not open to it. Their mind has not given itself permission to let that answer come in. It perceives it as an *attack* rather than a *blessing*. After all, isn't that what the universe does with ourselves?

How many opportunities for learning are present for us every day? A shelf full of lesson files to be pulled. And we walk, we look at them, we read their titles, and some days pull some. Some other days we walk right by them and pretend they are not there. Other days, after we have walked avoidant for a good while, the universe decides to let a folder fall at our feet.

We look around. We check for others looking our way and try to put it back on the shelf. Sometimes we succeed, without noticing that putting it back comes with a heavy price. We will be charged a *fee* for delaying that lesson. The universe is interconnected. The fact you are postponing learning the lesson now means others must stick around for when you decide to open that file.

Other times it is impossible to postpone the learning. Some of the agents of change involved are ready to move on.

They need to serve you *now*. You see the photos of all these people inside your folder, and the price that will be paid by not addressing it this time will accumulate.

Each of these people in your folder play a role, and it is to present the set of circumstances in which they can recreate a situation you must overcome. Each time you let one of these lessons go, and you don't get the movie, it turns more explicit, clearer, more painful. It is a call from the universe that you yourself have asked for.

When you finally decide to pull a folder and embrace its contents, celebrate. You will be overcoming a millenium of mistakes! Celebrate by being acceptant of your past, yourself and others.

Give them the mercy and the space they need to find their own moment of awakening. Bless them with the opportunity to choose their own time. To stand up and pick their next file from the shelf.

Affirmations of Power

I only have control over my
own destiny and purpose.

I *serve* others on their evolutionary
path by allowing them to face
their lessons at *their* own time.

I celebrate those entering and exiting
my life at the *exact* moment they do so.

Relationships: *Yourself* and the Other *You*

For many years I asked myself, am I in the right relationship? Is this relationship good for me? Am I good to my partner? At this point in my life, after many realizations have taken place, I wonder: was I seeing myself separate from my own relationship?

When you analyze the question my mind was asking above, can you see the two entities? Moreover, can you see how I was asking if the relationship was providing something to me? Is this relationship good to me?

I had no idea how I behaved in relationships. Had you actually stopped me and asked me about my beliefs, I would have come up with a really amazing concept for what a relationship is. Yet, that's not how my mind was responding to it. I would truly feel the heavenly concept of love within. But I could not see how my behavior would make me and others miserable. Even when attempting to correspond with my true beliefs.

I was waiting for the relationship to define me, and it did. Constantly. That means the state of the relationship defined my mood, my emotional state, and what I was able to happily give. When the relationship was not at its best, if those involved are not there to catch it, how could it survive?

I struggled to show up. I did, or at least I gave every piece of what I did not have, to show up. I believe I did show up many times, however, I did not enjoy it for the most part. If I served, I needed a response and feedback almost immediately. And of course, I did! I had given my last two cents. I needed a refund. And quick.

Serving others turned into a painful process. When I did, I would empty out instantly. I would stay there expecting, standing, hoping to be filled back. Like an empty bucket of shame.

I can clearly identify the pain right now. I can, with absolute certainty, identify what really hurt in those moments.

It hurt not *feeling emotionally able* to give to the person I loved, when it was what I wanted the most.

So here is a divine child of God struggling to love. Wanting to love and give, wringing every single drop from a heart that was empty.

Normally, an emotionally fit person in this situation would recognize there is an empty bucket there and say: Okay, I need to go fill this up, so I can serve you. I have to stop, go take care of myself, put my oxygen mask on, before I can be there for you.

But here is the essence of the matter. I did not recognize the lack as a problem within myself, but a problem in others.

Make *abundance* within yourself a *prerequisite* for your relationships. Your *lack* cannot be filled from an *external* source.

I was no one without the acceptance and validation of my partner. I could not stay still. I was anxious. I was terrified of my own state, of being alone with my thoughts. These thoughts that talked to me about what I had lived by and not who I was inside. I was terrified of not becoming who I heard I had to be, forgetting a small but very critical detail:

I should have set out myself to *accomplish* things in life, and not to *be* someone in life, for I already was. I had always been whole and nothing was ever missing.

This pattern was present my whole life, in all of my relationships. Romantically, in friendships. In some, stronger than others. But definitely more pronounced as I approached the realization of my absolute lack of self-love.

My marriage set me on the path for this transformation to take place. It gave me the necessary tools to experience my lack of self-love, over and over, and its consequences. Had I had an understanding and loving husband, I would still be light years away from the deepest realization of my life.

This is why I wrote this book. Many individuals already have an amazing mate. I had the *perfect partner* for evolutionary purposes, let's put it that way. I've shared these lessons with hope that it can inspire your heart to start searching for your ultimate fulfillment and true, giving love.

It took me a long time to realize my lacking. My mind, which still struggles with accepting the perfection of the universe, believes that if I had consciously known what I lacked, then I could have chosen to replenish sooner.

I would have built self-standards to be filled differently, in a loving way, or to step out with a little less overall damage. However, I feel not even one second was wasted. Every single experience had a purpose. All those experiences were used to be part of a destiny-changing decision.

Yet, I did not know I didn't love myself until I made the switch right in front of 5,000 other loving humans. When I experienced the love of so many others in the very moment I despised myself the most, it was in that moment I came to realize what was preventing me from living. It was my own neglect of my humanity.

How would our relationships change if we could see them as catalyzers to our wholeness and our contribution to the world?

The dominant question when facing a challenge was to doubt my partner, or the relationship itself: Is this relationship good for me?

What if we could ask a different question from now on instead?

How can I share even more the love and abundance that naturally occurs in my heart, in this moment?

Words of Wisdom

Stop for a moment.

Look at the relationships in your life. Is there any relationship that brings you pain, maybe discomfort? Are there any relationships you are hoping to change, improve or transform?

Improving our relationships is great. But consider that any change outside of your core and your emotional state is a change that will add anxiety to your life. Controlling anything external to you will add a great deal of stress to how you think and project toward yourself and others.

If we attach our realization to external agents, we might experience instantaneous successes and moments of pleasure, but would we experience fulfillment?

I see you.

I do not doubt your definition of love and relationship is quite beautiful and giving. We can love and even give our life for someone we love, yet fail to be happy ourselves. As a result, those who love us would also suffer. It's a no-winners game.

I invite you to look at how you define relationships and how much you really *enjoy* acting on that definition. Is it fulfilling? Or do you struggle keeping up with the definition of love you have set up for yourself? If you only have control of yourself (and partially!), can you really bet your daily energy on how the other person is having their day? Maybe only you exist in the universe, and me, and everyone, by ourselves. And from each of our solo perspectives everyone is an agent of change in each other's lives.

Thank the people in your life for being how they are. They will heal as you heal, they will have their own time to meet their lessons. Others will come who will challenge you with new lessons in life.

If you happen to lose perspective for a minute, look around you. Who surrounds you? Who are they? What challenges are you facing? Relationships are a way to serve others in their own destinies.

If you love others, *grow* so
you can set them *free*.

The deepest proof of love you can truly give is to act from your place of center and balance. It is a signal to the universe that you are ready to enter someone else's world, and make it worthwhile. If you do not love yourself, and you are in the search for the true you, the universe will serve you by bringing interactions with others who have the same need and even in a more pronounced way. It will bring you a mirror, bigger and clearer every time along the way.

Have you ever been to the optometrist where they show you the letters and numbers and ask you if you can see it now? And you can't? And they change the lens and repeat the question: can you see it now?

The lenses are our experiences. They get harder and harder for us to understand the picture we need to see of ourselves, and be able to decode it, read it, understand it.

Funny enough, I just got glasses.

Physical ones and emotional ones.

Get yours. Put them on.

Share yourself with others wearing them. Sharing who you really are is interacting from a vision and a concept of others that sometimes they cannot see. It is possible you will see two in every person you interact with. You might see their monster and their higher being. Their human nature, their lessons, and their heavenly presence. Your role is to interact with their higher selves, and love and appreciate their humanity.

> Do not engage negatively with the part of themselves they do not love.

Appreciate it, forgive it, and walk away from that door.

Face the other door, their heart.

Knock.

If they do not see their divinity, you must understand the shortest path to their awakening is just your presence. Gracefully wait at the door, with a full heart. Throwing rocks against that door will only thicken it, will only trigger more protection. Inside, there is a weak and thin being who is terrified to walk out. Only peace and love will make it safe to do so.

Wait for their bloom on the side of the door with open arms and a rose in your heart.

Affirmations of Power

I'm happy to *serve* those I cross paths with without *expecting* appreciation in return.

Everyone who enters my life is a *blessing* I have consciously or unconsciously *asked* for.

I open my *mind* and *heart* to interactions that match my *new* level of growth.

STEP FOUR

Learning to Love Yourself Completely

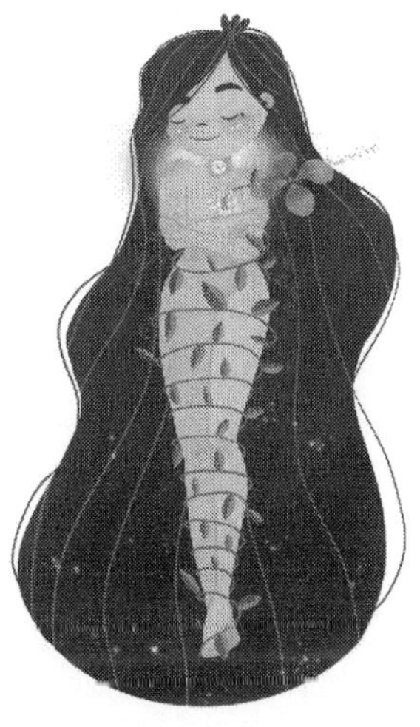

~ I stopped hiding from myself

and suddenly found me. ~

We explored the world of *others* and how to interact with them in a truly loving way. Yet I wonder, where is the limit between ourselves and the other human being, and at what point do we mistake love with excessive pleasing?

It is very important we learn that love and giving doesn't mean overlooking and rewarding negative and detrimental behaviors of others. That wouldn't be loving to them long-term. It is also not loving to yourself. It does not benefit anyone, yet it can be very hard to say no sometimes.

Let's explore the idea that our boundaries are there not only for ourselves, but for the benefit of others as well. And that when we drop our divine standards we are not serving the other person as a mirror they can model. We are not serving them by managing our own emotions so they can walk toward healing.

Let's explore a bit more about *self-love,* and how loving yourself is the most loving thing you can do for others.

Self-*love* is not Self-*ish*

I got this one wrong since the beginning. I don't remember when or how. But I had absolute certainty that loving myself was detrimental to others.

Growing up, in every single relationship in my life, this pattern emerged. With my friends and my romantic relationships. All permeated by the same limiting belief: *self-love is selfish*. Like all limiting beliefs, mine was followed by its corresponding threatening clause. If you spend time with yourself for *yourself*, you will be taking away from others.

I danced my way through life and love carrying along this pattern. What a heavy bag! I noticed later that carrying this belief cost me way more than failed relationships. I actually believed carrying it was not optional. It cost me my authenticity. And despite being a seeker of the truth, I became a vicious liar. The person I lied to the most—who do you think it was? Yep. You guessed right.

Me.

I lied to myself all the time. My biggest lie was to convince myself I was fulfilled and full of love. That I had plenty to give and share with those I loved the most.

> I believed that as long as I only lied to myself, everyone else would be *happy*.

This lack of self-authenticity manifested in my body. Think about it, a person who seeks and values the truth more than anything. A person who uses phrases like, "I'd rather die than lie." What do you think this behavior precipitated when I lied to myself?

Death.

When I was twenty-three years old, I faced thyroid cancer—located in the physical gland that corresponds to the throat chakra, which involves the ability to communicate one's truth, the art of self-expression, and clarity.

After I was given this diagnosis, I went through a couple of rough days. I questioned God and the purpose of life. This was three years before my conscious spiritual awakening. I was young and still dealing with the fear of God at this point in my life.

Somewhere between prayer and punishment, my whole existence was hanging by a thread. It was then that I asked myself, if I have to go now, what will I leave behind? I noticed that I hadn't started living. I didn't even know who I was, and I would never find out.

The notion of dying young made me see life differently. And I made decisions I thought I would never make. After all, the feeling propelling me forward was still fear.

In order to be on the safe side, I opted for a radical removal of the gland. I was terrified. At least it was one of the best cancers to have if I had to choose. The fact it had appeared at such an early age made me feel it had been a huge signal, a tremendous wake-up call.

For years I wondered if I had really healed. I knew I had taken the physical manifestation of the unknown cause out of my body, but I was not sure I had closed the leak up above. Was I still behaving in the same way that produced that effect in the first place? Was I just repeating the same mistakes all over again?

I could never really put my finger on what exactly it meant to have faced that challenge. I left it open and never felt completely healed.

Until now.

Today, I close a chapter in my life as I write this. It is one of the few in the handful of chapters I have closed in my existence. Today, I know I've found the answer and addressed internally the cause of that physical manifestation of pain and despair.

I'm healed.

Words of Wisdom

No more self-lies. No more artificial sweeteners. No more pretending to be edible and enjoyable to others. Grow to the beautiful feeling of absolute certainty that your raw-self is the biggest gift you can offer to the world.

Loving yourself *fully* is the biggest gift you can give to yourself and those you *love.*

There is beauty even in our most horrendous mistakes and programming. Can't you see how you were protecting others from the pain you feared the most? If it's life or death for you, would you want your loved ones to experience the pain you are trying to avoid? The answer is no, of course not!

So you protect them, protect them from the pain of not being fulfilled. But that pain is *your* pain! Not necessarily theirs!

It is common to attract a person who has the same lessons to learn as you. If they believe they lack, they will then take from what you give to them. They will try to take what you do not have either. This is the classic *empathic-narcissistic* relationship pattern.

They are both suffering. In the end, opposites in extremes are very similar in essence. They both lack the *self-love* and the *self-acceptance* they need. And that is essential to see the other person whole, complete, and not lacking. A divine son of God on their path on this earth.

Can you see how believing it is possible to take away from others, is to lock them into the same emotional jail you are in?

Freedom!
~ Tony Robbins

Can you see the projection? We push onto others what we suffer from. If you feel empty, you see them empty. And, if you are afraid to give to yourself because you won't have enough to give to others, can you ever truly receive?

This is what eventually makes us *unlovable,* even when being loved by others. We cannot feel the love, and we end up asking for more, and more, hoping we will one day feel like we dreamt it would feel. If we can never receive from those who love us, can we be part of a fulfilling relationship?

To love is to make a positive impact on someone else's life. What kind of impact can we make if we are in this infinite loop of misery?

Receiving with grace and enjoying it is the best gift we can give others.

> *Receiving* what we are given,
> is the best way to *reciprocate* love.

Appreciating what is being shared with us is a way to emotionally listen to those who are closer to our heart.

Love yourself, accept yourself, and forgive yourself for how you have behaved up to today. That is what you have done, but not who you are.

Loving yourself is a way to *free* others from having to *care* for your *unmanaged* emotions

When you finally stand up for yourself and feel love toward the human you are, your emotions fall into place. You are gifted with an understanding from above that will liberate you forever.

Affirmations of Power

I give myself permission *every day* to care and cater to the human being I am.

My best contribution to the world is my *own* healing and fulfillment.

I'm *worthy* of love, acceptance and understanding.

The Free World of *No Expectations*

I grew up with a scary set of expectations for myself. I must have dressed in them at some point along the way. And thank God for that! For these *expectations* kept me in check during my early twenties, while living by myself in a foreign country. They guided me to pursue good things in life. They kept me striving for excellence in my personal and professional life.

I had a very supportive family growing up. I still do! My parents were always there guiding and trusting me, but they never pushed me. I *pushed* myself. And I pushed hard. I got into good schools that require rigorous testing and academic standards at the age of thirteen. I went to boarding school when I was fifteen, and I was living by myself at the age of eighteen. From an early age, I was determined to achieve greatness, as far as I could see what greatness was.

Before I was diagnosed, I had not seriously considered marriage. As a matter of fact, I was one of those women who questioned marriage. I never saw myself having a happy marriage in any of my dreams. I was at a point in my life where I wanted to explore who I was, and get real about my true desires and goals. I was so young though, which is why now, as I look back, I can see the potential for problems. My innocence was almost intact and my heart was *flammable*.

This fire was extinguished the day I received my diagnosis. That day, any search lost meaning. Suddenly it wasn't about exploring feelings and having long and deep talks. Suddenly it got real. My mind freaked out, and I made sure to comply.

I started to build the life I had embedded in my unconscious as the perfect life. What I should do, the way it should be. I suddenly wanted a *husband,* not necessarily a *meaningful relationship*. I wanted a *functional home*, not necessarily a *happy* one, and children. I went for it, believing in the illusion that this *perfect new life* I was building would dissipate my inner battles and fear of death.

And you would say, well, what's wrong with wanting that life? What's wrong with building that kind of present for yourself?

The answer is, absolutely *nothing*. Where I went wrong was in designing that life within myself, and with no one else. My desperation was intense. I did not have time to explain and couldn't afford for others not to agree with my vision. I came up with the life I wanted and found the players who agreed to play the movie I had built in my head. And you can probably guess what happened next.

I expected to be a wife by twenty-five, I got married. I expected to own a home and have a family, and I did. I expected to be a mother by twenty-six, I had my beautiful son. But I also expected to be *happy*, and I wasn't. How could I possibly not be happy if I had met all my *expectations*?

Could it be those expectations and that model of a *happy life* weren't mine? If I had achieved the model in mind, and I wasn't feeling it, had I just built someone else's life thinking it would make me happy?

I discovered later on that I had stopped searching and inquiring about my soul's deepest desires. I had stopped looking for the love, connection, and relationship had I envisioned. This happened when my physical life was threatened. I had defaulted back to the recorded disk I had in my unconscious about *what life really is after all.*

I had gone back to those thoughts that stop us from growing. The limiting ones, the ones that make you settle. And when you stop searching deep, and stop daring to find your ultimate truth and purpose, you start living for the *outside* instead of the *inside.*

After all, you need to please *someone*. It's not you, and it's not your life anymore. So, we do a really good job of making sure others dream and desire the life we've built for ourselves.

One day I noticed how many of my expectations had materialized, but somehow, they did not feel mine. After all, they were just *met*, and not *created* by me.

Words of Wisdom

Expectations lead you to disappointment. Even if the expectation is met.

The disappointment is embedded on the *expectation* itself, not the *result*.

Have you stopped to think about that? Expecting means there is going to be some external stimuli that would bring some kind of change. It could be physical or emotional. Visible or invisible. Expectations are all over in our conscious mind, but also buried deep in our internal programming.

Have you noticed you *suffer* whether something you were expecting happens or it doesn't? You suffer a priori. You suffer because you wonder what will happen if things don't turn out the way you want.

If you are *expecting,* some of the ***power of creation*** you were naturally given is being transferred from *yourself* to external *circumstances*. Then we look at the failed outcomes and wonder how they did not materialize. Some of the *creation* and *manifestation* energy was transferred away, from the process of creation to *fear*. And sometimes the energy imbalance is not enough to materialize your dreams.

In the *absence* of fear, there are no expectations, there are *goals*.

Nothing wrong with dreaming. Nothing wrong with praying. Just be aware that those areas of your life that are still at the level of *prayer* and *dreams* will be your next *challenge*.

When we *dream,* we are eliciting from the universe the desire we need to put our focus in motion. When we *pray,* we are asking for the strength to face our own limitations.

Eventually they accumulate enough energy to propel a force of such magnitude forward that there is no question where you are going next. Those dreams become *goals*. Now they are *yours*.

Master the creation of your destiny by grabbing those dreams and consciously turning them into goals. Develop the awareness of the *gift* and the *blessings* you have even before the result is materialized and you will manifest *greatness* in your life.

Intensifying the potential of a dream with *gratitude* magnifies the transformation of energy toward the *manifestation* of a goal.

Gratitude is the catalyzer for that transformation. That's the secret to spark the reaction.

The act of being *grateful* for the opportunity of creating your own destiny in a *conscious* way is the action that turns your dream into a goal.

It replaces *fear*. It overcomes the difficulties of the mind. It opens your heart to defeat failure. This is the difference between motivational hope and trusting who you were meant to be. Here is where you consciously grab your life and make it *yours*, where you reclaim yourself for *good*.

Trade expectations for appreciation
~ Tony Robbins

Next time you have a dream, become aware of why it is a dream still and not a goal for you in your life.

When you are ready, give thanks for the awareness of that difference. Something magical will happen.

You will experience the true you, unfolding its power of creation and manifesting a walkable path to a new reality.

Affirmations of Power

Every dream of mine is a
goal in its *embryonic* state.

I consciously *manifest* each blessing in my
life by being grateful for its existence.

I *reclaim* the power of creation I was
given to turn my dreams into *reality*.

The *Essence* of Self-Love

Can you imagine what it is like to look back and not remember giving yourself to an experience, loving yourself enough to enjoy it completely? This is what I'm facing now in my life. I remember having loved so much. I remember giving myself fully and more. But I just remember the *hurt* and not the *pleasure* of it. This is because I gave all I had left, with the silent expectation of becoming myself.

When I look back *truthfully,* which is the only way I know how to look now, my human side wishes I would have approached those souls with a *full* version of myself. While it is very possible I wouldn't have become entangled with the same people if I had loved myself back then, the mind always wants to go back to the past and *idealize* an alternative future that differs from the present.

Man, I was hard with myself. And judged others by the same book as well!

I would give myself love when I achieved something phenomenal. I forgot to celebrate the small wins and the day-to-day blessings. A small bump in the road meant failure for me, followed by self-punishment, self-inflicted shame, and blame.

And the worst part? This would make me dress up my own results so I could talk about them in a loving note to others, expecting to get from them what I wasn't able to give myself. I do not know how to describe that more clearly than emotional jail. One I built for myself, or that I allowed myself to be in, simply because it served me. I did get a good amount of love for behaving this way. I think we all have at some point or another.

It's the *lie* we tell ourselves that determines how long we stay in a position of *comfortable* pain.

How was this going to help me wake up the next day to continue forward? My mornings got harder, my energy was depleted. I would cry at times just seeing my children play and running around because I didn't have the joy to share a moment of playfulness and happiness with them.

One day I realized I was becoming part of the same terrible force I gave my inner power to.

That day, the world shifted within me when I remembered the love I had once felt for myself, and most importantly, the love I could give to others because of the light I was able to channel through.

It was not a love that was always about to run out. It was not a love that needed *acceptance* and constant *reassurance.* It was a love that was free and would make me *soar* at the top of my destiny. A love that would give others the certainty of my soul's presence. In other words: *love.*

I do not blame anyone for having taken anything from me. No one did. What I lost sight of in my life, I gave away myself. I did this because it somehow accommodated me. It made me believe there was a shortcut to *self-love* that did not involve facing my deepest fears and the wounds of the past.

This experience of not loving myself, and having to walk from where I was toward self-love territory totally *naked,* it's the most unbelievable experience I could ever imagine. I thank those who crossed my path and gave their all to show me what emotional *misery* can be. For had I not been able to experience it, I wouldn't have been able to *overcome* it, and wouldn't be writing this book.

> What if your worst day was your best day?
> ~ Tony Robbins

I eternally thank Tony for his intervention, and for having allowed me to experience my own misery one more time. And my own crazy game of seeking *acceptance* and *acknowledgment* from others to validate my worth.

Only from the mud can you rise.

> Only if you are *dirty* can
> you wash yourself *clean*.

But Tony did more than that. He gave me a loving environment to experience the lesson. For I had pretty rough lessons in my life for many years, but there was no loving environment for me to undress my soul and know I would be supported, loved and cared for.

It is almost like being on life support for a moment, until you can let go of who you were and somehow get hold of the new human being you have become. It's a reconnection of the body, mind and soul.

The love I experienced at **Date with Destiny** was unmatchable. It was real. There was this instant in my life in which I experienced love from others, in the *absence* of self-love.

There was no confusion there. I was in a state of total despise toward my own existence, yet I felt the love from 5,000 souls, doing and teaching me how to do exactly what I needed to do. They showed me the path, for I saw them in their eyes.

I saw their own *pain* and the *braveness* of each soul loving themselves and standing tall in their own lives. I saw them being vulnerable and not reacting to people's feedback about how they were perceived. I saw them taking full responsibility for their own feelings and experience. I also saw their own acceptance of their failures. And their smiles.

I saw their strength and their grace at understanding that *authenticity* is the filter for relationships and the people we attract.

Real is better than *more*.

So I closed my eyes. I placed my right hand on my heart and walked toward an unfamiliar place within myself.

And I somehow liked what I found there.

Words of Wisdom

Get real with yourself. What do you really have otherwise? What can we experience from a place of self-doubt and judgment?

The memories we take with ourselves are the *true* feelings. Those truthful moments we shared with ourselves and others. If you do not give yourself *fully,* what kind of life are you really living? What kind of past are you hoping to remember?

Treasure the *authenticity* of each moment.

Some have to lie to themselves to remember a past they did not experience because they are not lovingly present in their lives at every moment. This limits them from connecting deeply in relationships. They are unable to connect with themselves. How can they connect with anyone else?

Connection is often mistaken by the *significance* you get when you expose a version of you that makes you comfortable.

But that pleasure lasts for as long as you can hold a fake smile. True realization and freedom come from the real love you experience after having made yourself vulnerable.

> The quality of your life is in
> direct proportion to the amount
> of uncertainty you can live with.
> ~ Tony Robbins

Your self-assessment is the validation that actually matters and registers within you at the end of the day. Regardless of the pleasure you might feel when others praise you, admire you or accept you, the only way you will experience a sense of fulfillment is when your own assessment matches theirs.

Their input never overrides yours for a long period of time. Soon enough, your own assessment comes crawling up from the caves of the mind, and you find yourself again dealing with your *monster* all over again.

The *essence* of self-love is to define yourself as *whole*, and love yourself completely as one *integrated* being.

We are the black and the white, the light and the dark, the yin and the yang.

Despising your dark side will not make you lovable. It's the opposite. It will attract those who, like you, despise theirs.

The relationship will then turn its attention to hide each person's dark side, and project a version of themselves they believe can be accepted.

Therefore, none of the parties would feel the love completely from one another, for they did not expose their real selves to be loved.

Affirmations of Power

The love I receive from others is
absorbed by the *totality* of my being.

I approve of myself and cherish
the journey that has made me who I am.

I love and give to *myself* with the same
intensity I love and dedicate to *others*.

STEP FIVE

Discovering Abundance Within

~ I turned my eyes inward and

found a whole new world out there. ~

Now that we have explored deeper our true nature, don't you wish you could tap into it more often? The light within you, what if we could find a way to keep it on?

Blackout periods in our lives will be less frequent. And when they occur, you will at least know how to light up the candle that will guide you to find the switch again.

The problem with the light is that we are too protective of it. We believe to have created it the first place. We confuse the blessing of being guided by our own entitlement for the blessings themselves. Our human nature steps in, and the light simply gets dimmer, and sometimes it goes off.

Let's dive deeper into the source of abundance we all have access to. Let's consider it is not a matter of *creating* blessings in our lives, but locating where the divine source of all creation is, and channeling the light through a flowing river of love.

If we find where abundance is, we will become the source itself.

Where the Heck Is *Abundance*?

Love thy neighbor as thyself.

Looks very pretty on paper. Right? For empaths, like the person I used to be, that phrase is nerve-racking. Love others as you love yourself. Do you mean I should treat others as badly as I treat myself? Because I do not love myself. Oh, wait, do you mean I don't love others either?

Empaths appear to love everyone and want to fix everyone's problems. This is their mechanism to feel validated and loved. They lack self-love. Their human motivation is to reach out to others and serve with the expectation to be loved back.

If I only do this, if I only do that, they will love me. They focus and make it about the other person until they are so depleted they break.

What I have come to realize along this journey is that we tend to believe about others what we ultimately believe about ourselves.

As you see yourself you will see *others*.

I started paying attention to this thought and the subtle idea of projection behind it. Soon I realized how skillful the mind is at softening your patterns.

The universe makes an effort to present you with lessons using others as mirrors every day. But the mind sneaks in and confuses the game with blame and projection.

Our first reaction when we see our bad traits in others is to repel them or to criticize them. Just like sometimes walking and seeing our reflection in a store mirror makes us snap and say: Oh! Who is that person?! In that same way, we emit judgments toward others, forgetting they are walking copies of our own features serving a divine purpose.

If I tell you how bothered I used to feel when people said: "Love from within," "Look inward," "Love yourself first," you wouldn't believe it. I just didn't know how to find abundance in me.

Loving someone for real should come from a deeper awareness of yourself and the other person. Just like you shouldn't need to spend the day at the spa to feel your self-love. It should be a deeper and gentler feeling of love that soften our interactions.

I knew I was a divine being, yet I was unable to tap into my divine power. I ran the other way for as long as I could until I faced the emptiest moment of my existence. There were no more doors around me, so I had to rise up.

I had to face the truth. As loving as I wanted to be to others, I had to give up my self-reputation as a loving person and accept I had come from a place of wanting to give in order to receive. Receive the very same feeling that was supposed to spark the love in the first place. Thus what I was giving was nothing more than a desperate cry dressed as a loving gesture.

The loving gesture would not dissipate as long as my technique worked out and I was being fed the love I craved. But when it wouldn't, my cry was loud and clear.

Words of Wisdom

Facing your truth is the most powerful moment you can have. That's where you *reclaim* your power. That's when you realize there was just so much about you that is untouched and ready to be discovered. It is an empty and lonely place where you can change your clothes, or better, take them off and dare to come back up. Naked.

Facing yourself is critical. Seeing your *monster*. Then there is something even scarier: Loving your monster. Please that guy once and for all, people! The monster will never give up his needs. It will dress up in white and fool you. You will find yourself saving the world in the name of the universe with the internal purpose of serving yourself selfishly.

When you tap into your inner power, that switches. Now you serve from a place of center that provides you with infinite resources. Because they are simply not yours.

When you are in a selfish state, you are your sole provider. You are saying to God, no, thank you, I don't need your resources, I can build it all for myself.

It's a spoiled child's attitude. Now you need a plan to rise up. After accepting you are in the deepest hole, denial won't prevent you from building an actionable plan.

Vitality, *joy* and *gratitude* are prerequisites for love.

Your energy, your body, your joy, and how grateful and aware you are of the blessing you already are today, is what is going to ignite the true source of unlimited love within you.

If you are struggling with staying full, stop. Take a break in your life, even if it is a private break for yourself. Take an emotional break as well. And think about replenishing the source of divinity within yourself.

You require energy to move around, to change your body, to be active. Make a plan for yourself that you can act on. What can you commit to today? What are the areas you could strengthen to reach a more pleasurable way to share the love you were already given when you were created?

Abundance is at the other side of *misery*.

Just as the darkest moment is a second before dawn.

There is no path to abundance.
There is a *switch* to abundance.

You will know when you arrive, for there is no *fear*. There is no way back to *emptiness*. There is no anxiety for losing the feeling of plenitude. There is no: "I hope this lasts." When you find it, you would have known you arrived forever. You will smile from a place of certainty that cannot be put into words.

Abundance does not need to be *replenished* for it does not *deplete* itself.

Abundance is the ability to channel your own light, which comes from the universe. It does not belong to you, it is not energy you generate from yourself. It is energy you find, and you learn how to channel it through you, to your inner world and to others.

Abundance is where true *fulfillment* comes from, and it can only be found *within*.

The universe always gives you back what you become. It mirrors your development. That's why all sorts of abundance will reach you as soon as you become it.

Sometimes we fear that giving from this abundant place will leave us with nothing. It's actually the opposite.

Becoming an *agent* of the light brings more light to our lives.

Get ready to experience an overflow of blessings: physically, emotionally, and spiritually, when you take the unbelievable step of facing and loving the scariest part of yourself.

Affirmations of Power

I find a universe of abundance *within* me
every time I'm caring and loving to *myself*.

I truly give to others when I do not
need *approval* for my loving actions.

I now love *boldly* and *fully*
from a place of plenitude.

Giving Is *Being*

I do not recall a time in my life when I wasn't crazy busy. I've been trying to accomplish the next thing while barely living. It is really interesting to me. As a matter of fact, I just realized something.

Since I set my first goal in my life, I have been in this chain reaction of things while trying to survive for the next one. For the first five years, I did pretty well. High energy, totally pumped with adrenaline. Enjoying the extreme high that being intellectually sharp produces in you. Reaching ten years, it had already started to take a toll on me. By the time I hit twenty years, I was so depleted and exhausted! It was obvious something needed to change in my life just for me to *stay* alive.

But what?

I kept thinking and thinking. I didn't do much more than come up with some new goals and new things to do. Hoping that when accomplished, my life would skyrocket.

And this is the promise I would make to myself every time. That the outcome of the goals I set for myself would somehow change the way I feel about things. But guess what, it instead controlled the way I felt about myself.

I overworked my own needs to the point of exhaustion. Trying to accomplish so I could finally be. I put my health on the line many times to help others succeed. I handled a business that wasn't mine. I worked on new projects and ideas for others. Implemented, re-implemented. Tried this, tried that. All with the purpose of getting the love and attention I really craved. All I got back were offenses and more demands. Never got the love I was *dying* to receive.

For years I would not get what I needed. Yet I kept listening to the demands of others and kept working toward my impossible goal. I did not realize back then that I needed to be first before I could even enjoy the smallest of the successes.

I had forgotten how to be myself.

By not being, I certainly could not love deeply and profoundly. I could not communicate my soul's desires and intentions. I had lost myself. I had allowed myself to drift away from my core purpose. I stopped being the person who people really loved, authentically.

Fast forward to the day in my life in which I became myself again. It was such a relief to be welcomed back! To be loved by me and feel the real love from others for the first time ever.

As soon as I returned to myself, this book's inspiration came to me, all at once, as I walked to my hotel room after the last session of **Date With Destiny**. Everyone was coming to me to give me a hug. Pouring so much love into my heart that I simply sat down and wrote a book in twenty-something days.

Can you imagine how long it would have taken me to write a book if I had decided I wanted to become an author and started fishing for book ideas? It could have been as fast, sure. But certainly, I would have had to push myself a lot to make it.

I soared through this journey because I became *it* before I executed it. I crossed through the life lessons needed for the outcome to fall into my lap. And that's where you see the magic of the universe unfold in front of your eyes.

So I sat and watched. And looked up to heaven and thanked my own soul for this incredible opportunity to be aware of the light we've been given.

Words of Wisdom

Think about a goal in your life right now. What would happen when you achieve it? Why is achieving so important to you? It is amazing to work for goals, but do you celebrate your life, your success?

What would you do when the race is over? When you notice the exhausted, unfulfilled version of you is still waiting for you to show up? Are you pushing to get things done or are you soaring through your destiny while you work hard?

You need a quick shift of focus. A shift that generates unlimited energy for you and your projects. You won't need to push so hard to achieve things.

It might even feel that you have to carry yourself around from place to place. As if the emotional you had to convince itself over and over of the reasons you are doing something. I know it feels that way sometimes. And you push through it telling yourself it will be different this time.

You tell yourself that this time something new will happen. Someone will finally understand and notice your hard work, and then you will relax. Then you will take care of yourself, finally! But that never happens, does it? And you are at the end of your rope.

You might be even turning on yourself and starting to behave like the person you never wanted to be. You feel you need to stop but can't seem to figure out where to go from here.

Imagine you could tell yourself to walk and you would just go! Imagine if you could align that mind with that body, and your body would simply respond to your inner plan.

What is that part of us that *resists* and doesn't follow? Somehow, along the way, you tried to get rid of your internal enemy. Someone rejected you for a human trait you exposed and you classified it as not good. You marked it for deletion.

This is an unconscious process we all have running inside. We have been on the lookout for this internal enemy and been on a mission to destroy it.

This is the side we attempt to hide from others. We hide one side of us, the one we hate the most. Don't get rid of the enemy within, because even that is suicide.

Acknowledge it, love it. For meeting its needs is what you are missing to finally accept yourself. You will then stop looking for what you have been desperately seeking from the outside world. You will instead turn inward to meet your deepest needs.

When you are at your *center*,
the conflict *ends*.

Now what you do flows. It doesn't matter how difficult it could be, or how big the goals might be. You are now flying at the top of your wings. Now the goals pull you. You are truly attracted to your own life, your family, and others.

You are going to feel like gravity has become lighter, for you will be floating in the ecstasy of realization and deep understanding.

Stop doing to *be*.
Be, so you can really *do*.

The shift in focus is, in essence, the realization you will double, triple what you can do and achieve if you show up fully all the time. When you do not have to spend daily energy getting yourself to buy into your life again and again. Who wants that anyway?

Imagine you have to jumpstart your car every single day. For the first month, it's not a big deal, then you start hating it while telling yourself how grateful you should be you have a car in the first place. This is the internal conflict which stagnates us.

This feeling of having to drag yourself and, at the same time, feeling guilty for wanting more, can be applied to many areas of our lives. Even if you are extremely wealthy. If you achieved that success pushing yourself, you must have struggled through life. You might be proud of it, and that's how you allowed yourself to love you, and others might love you for it as well.

But are you fulfilled?

Trust me when I say you could have experienced more love and more satisfaction than what you have experienced up to this point. And it basically comes from the freedom of not expecting love, acceptance and appreciation as a reward for your achievements.

It's not that you won't have it, but rather that you give yourself the love, acceptance and appreciation before you go on the quest for success.

Giving is being.

From now on, you walk into goals with the love, the acceptance and the appreciation you thought you would receive when the goal was completed.

This is why visualization works. People imagine the result, and they tell you: *feel like you would feel when the goal is achieved*. The key word is to feel. It's not like some magic is going to happen and things will be suddenly done for you. It is that you are going to celebrate right now. You are happy now. You solve the conflicts that take energy away from the project before you start the project. You become whole and fulfilled just by having the chance to pursue the dream.

So now you know.

If you want to do X, become X, and the universe will conspire to make it happen.

Become your most precious desire. Then sit and watch how you will flow through your goals, and the hard work would be the marvelous journey you envisioned it would be.

Go become, and let's get doing.

Affirmations of Power

I love myself *wholly*.

My body, mind and soul engage as one in the pursuit of my dreams.

I become what I want to achieve.

Contribution and *Evolution*

Twenty days ago, contribution seemed so far away. I never thought I would get there. It felt like something great people would do to look good, but faked to enjoy. Such were the limitations in my head. I couldn't even succeed at contributing to those closer to me, imagine for others!

Now obviously, my thoughts were all mixed up. Conceptually and emotionally. I believed I was contributing to others when in reality I wasn't.

I was giving everything I had, which was pretty little, to get the love and appreciation in return. And I wasn't interested in getting love from people I didn't even know, so why contribute? I do not know of anything more selfish than this *(pause)*. This is such a shame.

But today I'm not ashamed of it, for this is how I behaved, but not who I am.

It is important to dwell here for a minute. To understand as much as possible about what it really means to *give*. The realization of selfishness is what has liberated me and has me soaring to my new destiny. The destiny quietly waiting for me.

I had a phenomenal experience last night. I did not anticipate it or plan it, but I happened to notice how it felt. It was completely unexpected.

I got invited to attend a women's dinner where we met to talk about deeper subjects. Love, courage, fear, things of that sort. And how women face and overcome those in their lives.

First of all, the old me would never have shown up for this dinner. I would never have booked it in the first place! It would have been considered by my husband *a way to spread energy outside of the marriage*. And I would have happily obeyed, because to me, deserving his love was definitely worth giving up my own life.

This time, I not only booked it, but I happily coordinated care for my children so I could focus that afternoon and attend. At that point, I still hadn't realized how everything was different. I was happy and excited to attend a dinner with other people I did not know and be myself! Wow! I consciously did not realize this until the dinner was over and we were sharing our final thoughts.

I suddenly felt like I belonged, and that I had created a bond with other women for the first time. This was a gift I wasn't expecting. It was a reaffirmation of my healing.

I did not propitiate this experience. Consciously, that is. But I welcomed it. And that was one of the biggest gifts I have received lately.

We all spoke during the dinner. Eventually, it was my turn. I had listened to each of the shares, and the feeling of doing for others while feeling unappreciated was common for everyone at the table.

I spoke about myself, and about the old me.

About how there was a time I believed I was being wronged by others, mistreated and not appreciated. I opened up and shared about how being wronged, mistreated and unappreciated for real was something I chose because it served as a refuge for my lack of self-love. And most of all, because it confirmed my self-treatment.

I spoke about my desire to give to others, when in reality, it was my ego dressed as a giving person to elicit the love I wasn't giving myself.

Yes. I spoke and told everyone how, despite the horrible treatment of my husband, I put myself in a situation in which he could mistreat me.

I spoke about my codependency.

I spoke about my empathic personality combined with an extreme lack of self-love, and how it was detrimental to my life.

But I also spoke about how I rose up from the ashes.

I expressed the amazing moment in which I became myself again, and how I had found my internal balance. It was then when I realized I was finally contributing something to others. Not by being perfect and spotless, but by being me.

Real is better than perfect because it's *you*.

So I gave what I had. And this time, when I was done, I had more than I initially had for myself.

This is the most incredible feeling of all.

This is true *freedom*.

I'm at the doors of *contribution* now. This book is my first act of giving to myself and others without expecting anything in return.

It feels damn good.

Words of Wisdom

What would it take to get to the end, to the limit of yourself? When would you have given enough to yourself and realized it hasn't taken you to where you want to get?

At the end of yourself is *others*.

Sadly, only pain makes us rise from our own misery. When it hurts the most, when we have lost something very dear to us.

Where are you in your life right now? Have you really crossed the limit of the pain of not being yourself? Have you had a dark night of the soul yet? If you have, you have also most likely had the beautiful sunrise that follows.

The ancient masters once said that our evolution in this world resembles a spiral staircase. They say we grow and evolve as if we were climbing the stairs, one step at a time.

Each step is a lesson we face, and every time we lift our whole body and carry on to the next step, it's a new beginning, a new awakening.

At the end of *each* step, there is a dark night of the soul, a moment of *deep* introspection and *connection.*

Notice all the effort is done right in that moment of the step up.

As we are in one step, we walk flat, we are presented with parallel events and things that give us all the tools we will need for the final lesson.

We then face it when it presents itself, and have to rise up considerably to take the next step forward.

Change happens in one moment.
~ Tony Robbins

Notice also a very interesting detail. What does the spiral mean? Why that symbol, and how does it relate to evolution and growth? Why spiral and why not ascending in one direction only?

The revelation behind this analogy is the fact that we do not only overcome lessons in one level of awareness. We overcome these lessons at many levels of the unconscious.

Have you noticed also how we are often presented with the same lesson but at a higher level? Somewhat harder, deeper, more challenging?

Yes. I'm sure you have experienced this as well. And it is really important to recognize when this happens, and not mistake it for having failed a previous lesson.

Sometimes we overcome a situation, and we are doing better, and suddenly, we are hit with what it seems is the same wave of consequences.

In this moment, stay still. Repeat your lesson. Be aware you are testing yourself one more time. Maybe to discover a new detail, a new breakthrough to expand your previous awareness.

Growth is repetitive but never *redundant.*

The importance of staying still and trusting the ways of the universe to accomplish things are critical for steady evolution.

Here is what happens when we sometimes interfere in the divine order of things. In the end, everything will be fine. The universe reorganizes if you spoil its plan. Yet, that energy spent in reorganizing must be put back. That's why sometimes we add unnecessary suffering to our lives.

About Causes and Effects

Ancient knowledge says that cause and effect dance together under a universal law. Just like everything else does. You, me, your neighbor. Everything and everyone. The sea, the planets, the stars. Undermining the order and the power of the universe is almost silly. Everything that happens in life has a cause, a moving force which started it.

A *cause* will always unleash an *effect*.

Eventually, that is. Because we really do not know when it will materialize. We put a cause in motion, often without realizing. And we get effects reflected back to us. We often mistakenly match the effect to the wrong cause. And if it goes against our plans, we call the universe unfair, and we get discouraged, angry even.

Between *cause* and *effect* there is a *lag*.

This lag is what gives us that unknown void space in which the causes get detangled from their effects. We sometimes do not know what triggered what.

When you get an amazing reward from the universe, have you caught yourself wondering what you did that precipitated such a blessing?

Exactly. In the same way, we send out negative causes, and we often fail to match the unfortunate results to the real cause which unleashed it.

But there is something even more eye-opening. Something we do know. The universe guarantees that:

Each effect will have the
same polarity as its cause.

This means if we put in motion a positive cause, a positive effect is guaranteed to make its way to us. We do not know when exactly, but you bet it will. The same thing happens with a negative cause. A negative effect will reach our lives, eventually, matching its initiating cause.

But that is not it. The law says something even more interesting. The *lag* between cause and effect is called ***manifestation***.

Manifestation will have an *opposite* polarity to the cause and effect.

What does this mean? It's what you have heard your whole life in the streets.

Good things happen to good people, but they struggle a whole lot. And someone who did something wrong might be enjoying it right now, but sooner or later, they will pay for what they did.

Does that make sense? Someone trying to achieve a positive goal that will benefit many people will most likely have a deep and dark manifestation. Many obstacles, a lot of tests, but in the same magnitude, the effect will present as big, if not bigger, than it was envisioned.

Always remember this:

The Universe is *exact* for the lesson to meet its purpose, but is *generous* once the lesson is learned.

The manifestation is a moment of *reflection,* of looking inward. It is a chance for the cause to be repaired.

For the *negative* causes, it is a chance to *redeem* yourself.

To say: Even though I'm currently enjoying the benefits of my wrong action, I will go back and fix the cause I put in motion in the first place.

For the *positive* causes, it is a test of *perseverance.*

Are you really committed to supporting this light in the world? The universe says: I will send you struggles to test your determination.

In both cases, we often crumble and fail. Sometimes we do not take back negative actions, and sometimes we take back positive ones. In any case, we struggle to match the effect to its cause. Especially when the manifestation is long.

So what do we do? In the spirit to fix things, we impulse another cause instead of making a correction or sticking through the manifestation. When life hurts or becomes difficult, we set free another cause. In the middle of the manifestation we change course, we go with plan B, without knowing the universe is working hard for plan A to manifest. And the infinite recursive loop is so deep by now that knowing why things are happening the way they are is truly a guessing game.

Staying *still* through the manifestation of your positive causes is a skill you must develop.

This is one of the reasons I stood still through Tony's intervention. It was painfully beautiful. It hit the core of the pain accumulated for centuries.

But I knew my heart wanted healing. True healing. True love. I trusted that with absolute certainty.

I knew then that an amazing effect would unleash. I was certain. I have never been more certain in my life.

As I was crying with Tony's team by my side, I looked up and saw the sky full of stars. I was so breathtakingly happy.

I told everyone holding my hand in the sacred circle of the blessing that I was the luckiest person on Earth.

I didn't know why, or how, but that moment, and sticking through that moment, was the biggest blessing of my life.

And here I am.

Affirmations of Power

I'm fulfilled, therefore I give.

I embrace the lessons that seem to *repeat* in my life and understand they are just there to *strengthen* my divine nature.

I await and trust that the universe will always send back an *effect* with the same polarity as my *intentions.*

Final Words

Stepping into authentic healing feels absolutely peaceful. It is an interesting *peace*. It is not a peace of no conflict. It is a peace of having a conflict that resolves.

Handling healthy, loving conflict and achieving resolution is a skill we must develop and eventually master. From a place of self-love, which translates to a place of loving others, conflict resolution is perfectly attainable.

The dance between two souls, two humans, is a sacred dance. Every interaction is holy. When someone is able to be your loving mirror, your light will shine so brightly that it might make you spark into a whole new level of yourself. *That* is love.

The biggest lesson I learned from this journey to my real self was to understand we must function as two beings.

We must be the ***maestro*** and
the ***disciple*** at the same time.

We just need to recognize what we are called to be in each situation life presents to us.

Most of the time, we spend a great deal of energy assessing and trying to fit ourselves into a category, in a level on our path. And we struggle to fix the needle into a set position.

So the next experience comes, and we fail. We can't behave quite as the *maestro,* so we reassess . . . and we lose focus . . . reassessing . . . asking what we are . . . and the process repeats.

We judge, we suffer, and we don't forgive ourselves. We drive further and further from the lesson itself, caught up in this insane wave of self-evaluation.

The biggest takeaway from this unbelievable journey was to learn that life is eternal, there is not a set current state of being, but a set current state of circumstances which define a lesson. And in that lesson one can be appointed to be the teacher or the student. And in both I'm serving my divine brother or sister, only from two different perspectives. This has liberated me from a pain I never knew I was carrying.

In a recent meditation, a sensation of falling asleep due to total physical exhaustion took over. It was followed by a strong sense of awakening. I felt forced to breathe in deeply, way deeper than I can normally breathe in. I felt an *ascension,* as if someone was taking me by the hand, higher.

Tears reached my eyes, because very rarely have I felt something as genuine as this. A friendly touch in the soul that cannot be described. It is a sense of companionship which cannot be matched. I've had very few experiences like this that I'm aware of, but I can distinguish them by the lack of solitude.

I'm certain those who have felt this know what I'm referring to. This was accompanied by a very clear revelation.

There was a *candle* and a *mirror* in this vision. I learned while receiving this impression that the mirror not only receives the light but also reflects the light it receives. I realized we are not the candle or the mirror, I realized we are both. The candle *and* the mirror.

> This is the spiritual *oscillation* which allows for self-contemplation and *real* self-evaluation.

I realized that connecting with another human being requires the sensitivity to know what you need to be in each particular moment. And what matters to the universe is the light reflected in the total interaction! The energy of the reaction!

I realized, with the divine help of the masters, that:

Two mirrors, do not *produce* light, and
the light of two candles is never *reflected*.

Applying the Five Steps In a Quick Thought

You can exercise the five steps in a quick cycle, every day, every time you need to. A simple thought can have the power to bring you back into a state of awareness.

When a feeling of being unappreciated or unloved comes back to haunt you, remember that the first rejection might have come from your own self. You have transferred the power of your own happiness to others. To something external to yourself.

Take back your life and automatically enhance your interactions with the other human beings around you by freeing them from the responsibility of having to "make you feel" a certain way.

BREAK FREE from the mental fog that has you in a victim position. Whatever you are going through has a purpose, and a solution.

FORGIVE YOURSELF for having gotten there, for having believed that someone else is responsible for what has happened to you.

SEE OTHERS for who they really are. Understand they have a journey of their own. That they are also human, that they suffer, and that they might have less awareness than you currently have.

LOVE YOURSELF first, and completely, by accepting your human nature.

FEEL THE ABUNDANCE the Universe has given you access to.

Open your eyes and tune into the heart and soul of other humans around you.

Do you feel them yet?

Acknowledgments

The incredible Tony Robbins and Sage, his wife, for having put together this *thing* called Date With Destiny. His team of outstanding individuals and amazing agents of change and light. I love you, thank you.

To the 5,000 souls present at Date With Destiny Florida 2018. Thank you for sharing your light and energy so I could heal. I'm in awe of your generosity and your incredible love and support.

To my three children, for having kept me sane, centered, and focused. For showing me that life is always worth living despite the suffering we might experience at times. I adore you all.

My supportive soul companions, and my *dad.*

Mingo Scordo, a big eternal piece of my heart. Thank you for lifting me in the moments of disbelief for over 16 years, and for reminding me that love is always worth growing for.

My ex-husband. Thank you for all the *human* pain and all the *lessons,* for I have been rewarded with much *light, awareness,* and *wisdom* once I stepped toward *real* healing.

Aura Ilustrada

To the incredible Laura, whom, with so much *love* and *intuition,* channeled my journey's representation in the form of images as a beautiful gift to me and the world. Thank you *@aura_ilustrada*